## PRAISE FOR FUTURE CHURCH

I remember watching Terry Parkman pour his heart into our students week after week, reaching hundreds of young men and women. Terry didn't just lead a youth ministry—he led a movement, pastoring an emerging generation with vision, compassion, and bold creativity. Now, in *Future Church*, Terry puts into words what he lives out through the local church. What I love most about this book is that it's more than a strategy guide—it's a call to courage. It invites us to stop fearing disruption and start stewarding it for Kingdom impact. If you've ever wondered how the Church can remain faithful to the Gospel while engaging the next generation in a rapidly changing world, this is the book you need in your hands and in your heart.

—DOUGLAS M. GRAHAM, DMIN
Former President, North Central University, Minneapolis; Former Lead Pastor, Evangel Assembly of God, Bismarck, North Dakota

*Future Church* is a prophetic, passionate, and practical call to align with what God is building in the next generation. I have watched Terry up close and personal as he has challenged our team to move from preference to purpose, from preservation to pursuit. This book isn't about tweaking yesterday's church—it's about empowering tomorrow's leaders to carry the fire of revival with clarity and conviction. If you care about where the Church is going and you want to see the road map, you need to read this book!

—PASTOR ROB KETTERLING
Lead Pastor, River Valley Church, Minnesota

Because the Church is the primary agency that God uses to expand His Kingdom here on earth, Dr. Terry Parkman takes us on an optimistic journey in *Future Church* to show how young, vibrant leaders can keep the Church missional and effective amid all the rapid societal changes. For those giving their lives to build Christ's Church, this is a must-read.

—Doug Clay
General Superintendent, Assemblies of God (USA)

In *Future Church*, Terry Parkman offers a prophetic and practical road map for navigating the seismic disruptions transforming our world. With a deep commitment to the next generation, Terry calls the Church to embrace change for Kingdom impact. His message is timely, urgent, and full of hope. This book is a must-read for every leader who desires to see Generations Z and Alpha and beyond reached and rise as pioneers of the Gospel.

—Dr. Billy Wilson
President, Oral Roberts University; Global Chair, Empowered21

There is unprecedented change for the youth and young adults within our societies, but there is also a season of spiritual renewal and interest such as seen in the UK's Quiet Revival. In *Future Church*, Terry Parkman, a globally respected and loved pastor and a researcher focused on emerging generations, provides a prophetic and clarion call to those of us who are parents and leaders in the global Church. He gives voice to the young men and women in Gen Z and Gen Alpha who indicate God is doing things that our structures may not be made for. He appeals to us to be malleable and quick responders to the work of the Spirit and the opportunities we are experiencing for relational, truth-based discipleship. As we do, watch the future church go way beyond anything we've seen before.

—Rev. David Wells, MA, DD
General Superintendent, Pentecostal Assemblies of Canada;
Vice-Chair, Pentecostal World Fellowship;
Chair, PWF Christian Unity Commission

When it comes to learning about Generations Z, Alpha, and Beta from a global perspective, Dr. Parkman is the expert I want to learn from.

In *Future Church*, he presents God as "the Original Disruptor," a title that becomes the battle cry for a church. The body of Christ refuses to retreat in fear of change but celebrates a faith that, age after age, has proved to be resilient and creative while being firmly anchored in Christ's truth. If you want to learn how to harness disruption in the Church, this is the book to read.

—Dr. Esteban Solís
Lead Pastor, Iglesia el Centro Costa Rica

Dr. Terry Parkman has written the book the Church desperately needs right now. He doesn't just diagnose the seismic shifts happening around us—he also provides a road map for navigating them with biblical wisdom. Terry helps us see disruption not as a threat to be feared but as an opportunity to be embraced. Rather than retreating into nostalgic models, he challenges us to seek the prosperity of our digital Babylon while remaining anchored in the Way. This isn't another book lamenting how technology is destroying the Church. Instead, it offers strategies for discipling Generations Z and Alpha in ways that honor both their digital nativity and their hunger for authentic encounters with Jesus. This book will be an essential guide for the Church in the digital age.

—Pastor Becky Johnson
Lead Pastor, Jesus Culture Sacramento

Dr. Terry Parkman is one of the world's leading voices on navigating the future of discipleship and reaching the next generation. This groundbreaking work, produced out of the deep research journey of his doctorate, carries the weight of historical reflection, prophetic insight, theological depth, and carefully considered practical wisdom. *Future Church* is more than a book—it's a rallying cry to the pioneers, the Issachar generation, those who discern the times and refuse to let the gospel get lost in translation. In *Future Church*, Terry doesn't just analyze disruption—he teaches us how to harness it for revival. If you're serious about equipping and leading the next generation into the future and seizing the opportunity the Lord is placing before us, *Future Church* is essential reading.

—Layla Nahavandi, MA, MTh, PhD (Cand.);
Founder and Director, The Burning Hearts Movement

Dr. Terry Parkman is a pioneering voice for this generation—his thought leadership reframes disruption not as a threat but as an invitation for the Church to adapt, disciple, and lead with bold clarity. I've always admired how Terry blends theological depth with cultural discernment, challenging us not just to think differently but to move differently too. In a world where truth is often shaped by trends and filtered through emotion, Terry anchors us in the unchanging Gospel and invites us to disciple the emerging Church with both strategy and Spirit. *Future Church* is more than a book—it's a prophetic blueprint to raise up resilient, Spirit-empowered leaders who will carry the mission of Jesus into every corner of this Adaptive Age.

—Andy Kirk
ACC National Leader, Kids Ministry

As someone leading youth and young adults in an increasingly digital, distracted, and posttruth culture, I found *Future Church* both confronting and life-giving. Terry writes with the urgency of someone who's been in the trenches and carries a prophetic burden for the next generation. This book helped me see disruption not as something to fear but as something God can use to advance His Kingdom. It's deeply relevant, full of insight, and packed with practical handles for anyone serious about discipling Gen Z and Gen Alpha. Whether you are leading a church, are leading a youth ministry, or just love the next generation, read this. It'll shift the way you see the future.

—Rev. Andrew Yeo
Executive Director, Festival of Praise Singapore

*Future Church* is a strategic, prophetic blueprint for Christians as we navigate the turbulent waters of generational change, cultural disruption, and technological advancements that will impact the current and future Church. Terry Parkman's book carries deep biblical insight, practical wisdom, and a historical understanding that helps us understand a new and faith-filled approach to growing and empowering the next generation of the Church. Every page of this book will challenge you to upgrade your leadership to lead in a culture where faith is tested, truth is relative, and the next generation is under assault. This book is a field guide for the journey ahead of you and a catalyst for us as church leaders as we lean in to courage, curiosity, and the power of the Holy Spirit to disciple a generation that will lead us into the future of the Church.

—SHARON WITTON
Co-Lead Pastor, Toronto City Church

Terry is one of the leading voices in this space in our generation. He unfolds the riveting story of how AI, Web3, the metaverse, and all their friends are unapologetically shaping our global culture while powerfully charging the Church to unapologetically engage our young people on how to live, express, and radiate Jesus in this new world. It's nothing short of shocking! Each chapter reveals the reality of our fast-changing world—not with fear but with fierce hope that the Church need not be sidelined. We can either resist the change or press in to redeem every bit of it. Whether you're a church leader in Lusaka, Zambia, or a pastor in Denver, Colorado, this is a NextGen field manual for the Church of tomorrow—and the day after. Parkman speaks from the depths of his experience, painting a vivid picture of urgency, and then boldly reaffirms the ancient and current relevancy of Jesus. This is a compelling charge to the Church to see the spaces of AI, the metaverse, and Web3 as territories for redemption—not retreat zones—and to not flinch on the never-ending relevance of the Truth. This book equips pastors and leaders to navigate the cultural and technological shifts with bravery and fortitude and to do more than survive them—to lead within them. Say goodbye to top-heavy Christian clubs and hello to a bold era of brave discipleship. Web3 and decentralized systems may try to redraw the maps of meaning and identity, but they can never replace the power of authentic, Spirit-led discipleship.

—TOMMY DEUSCHLE
Pastor, Celebration Churches International; Founder, CMedia Africa; Founder, celebrateAmusic

It has been said that the one constant in life is change! Change can feel overwhelming, but it is also full of possibility and growth. *Future Church* by Terry Parkman provides a clear and practical guide for navigating the challenges of a changing culture that the modern world and this present day present. This book is essential for any leader wanting to engage with Generations Z and Alpha and future generations, empowering and releasing them to become Gospel strategists and Kingdom pioneers.

—Tony Stewart
First Assistant General Overseer, Church of God, Cleveland, Tennessee; Lead Pastor, Citylife Church, Tampa, Florida; Empowered21 Chair—USA Cabinet

Disruption is viewed through two lenses: fear or faith. While ignorance can fuel fear, knowledge deepens faith even in the face of an uncertain and disruptive future. Terry reminds us disruption demands pioneers. This book will equip you with insight, understanding, and wisdom to pioneer again and lead courageously—relearning how to fulfill the Great Commission in this unprecedented era of change.

—Julius Rwotlonyo
Lead Pastor, Watoto Church, Uganda

*Future Church* is a powerful and practical guide for anyone passionate about reaching the next generation. Terry brings clarity and conviction to the conversation in a way that's both inspiring and actionable.

—Vince Parker
Lead Youth Pastor, Life.Church

*Future Church* by Terry Parkman is not just a book—it's a prophetic, pastoral invitation to reimagine what it means to be the Church in the age of algorithms, AI, and adolescent spiritual hunger. Terry doesn't fear disruption—he names it, honors it, and reminds us that God has always used it as a holy tool. In a culture moving faster than our liturgies can catch up, Parkman calls leaders, parents, and pastors to slow down and listen to the digital generations with ears tuned to both culture and the Kingdom. It's as if he's gathered us around a fire and said,

"Look. Pay attention. Don't miss what God is doing here." He's writing to a weary, wondering Church, one that aches to remain faithful even as the familiar forms fall away. And through every page, he invites us to trade nostalgia for vision, resistance for wisdom, fear for formation. If you're feeling disoriented by the noise of the now and unsure how to disciple the next, *Future Church* will meet you right where you are—and gently usher you toward where the Spirit is leading.

—ANDREA LATHROP
Senior Vice President, OneHope

*Future Church* is a practical guide for leaders navigating the cultural complexities and disruption of our time. With visionary depth and clarity, this book (or Terry) reframes discipleship, challenges institutional drift, calls the Church back to its missional essence, and provides a blueprint for catalytic action.

—JENN BROWN
Vice President of Collaborative Partnerships, OneHope

For years Terry has been a leading voice on generational trends in the Church. What sets him apart is his ability not only to anticipate future shifts but to leverage them for the growth of the local church. In *Future Church*, he offers insight into the disruptions upcoming generations will face—along with practical tools the Church can use to adapt to an ever-changing culture. He helps the Church stay mission focused while emphasizing the need to evaluate and adjust our methods. *Future Church* is a valuable resource for any leader committed to discipling the next generation and harnessing its adaptive nature to build the Church.

—AUSTIN WESTLAKE
National Youth Director, Assemblies of God USA

Terry Parkman is one of the leading voices on NextGen ministry in the global church. He has correctly identified the season of disruption in which we are living and its huge potential for advancing the Gospel. God is setting the stage for an unprecedented revival among

Gen Z and Gen Alpha. I pray that we are wise enough to listen to the message of *Future Church* and embrace what the Holy Spirit is doing around the world.

—Ashley Wilson
Global Executive Director, Empowered21

In *Future Church*, Terry Parkman powerfully reframes disruption as divine opportunity. He challenges us to see today's cultural and technological shifts not as threats but as waves the Church can ride to reach and empower the next generation. This is a must-read for leaders ready to move with God in a changing world.

—Daniela Freidzon McCabe
Pastor and Speaker, King of Kings Church, Argentina

There are many voices speaking about youth and discipleship, but Terry Parkman is one you need to hear. This book is not just theory—it's about strategy and system to empower and disciple young people. His passion for Gen Z and Gen Alpha is only matched by a clear blueprint for how the Church can grow stronger and younger. If you're ready to move beyond inspiration and aspiration into real implementation, *Future Church* is a must-read.

—How and Lia
Founding Senior Pastors, Heart of God Church, Singapore; Authors, *GenerationS: How to Grow Your Church Younger and Stronger*

# FUTURE CHURCH

## *HOW DISRUPTION, INNOVATION, AND A NEW GENERATION ARE RESHAPING THE CHURCH*

**TERRY PARKMAN, DMin**

FOREWORD BY ROB HOSKINS

SPERO
HOPE FOR THE WORLD

FUTURE CHURCH: HOW DISRUPTION, INNOVATION, AND A NEW GENERATION ARE RESHAPING THE CHURCH



Published by Bible Media Group LLC
biblemediagroup.com

Manuscript prepared by Kyle Duncan
Cover design by Joe DeLeon



ISBN: 979-8-9929376-4-0 (Paperback)
ISBN: 979-8-9929376-8-8 (Ebook)

Printed in the United States of America

10 9 8 7 6 5 4 3 2 1

*For Christina:*

*Your unwavering love and support have carried me through every chapter of this journey. Thank you for believing in the call long before these words were ever written.*

*For Avalie and Nova:*

*This is written with your generation in mind—that you might inherit a Church ready for the world you're called to lead.*

# Contents

## PART II: WHERE WE ARE

## PART III: WHERE WE ARE GOING

# Foreword

We are standing at the edge of massive disruption.

The ground beneath our feet is shifting—technologically, culturally, and spiritually. The ways people engage with truth, form identity, and pursue purpose are being rewritten in real time.

Yet God is not surprised. Every great move of God throughout history has emerged through times like these, when old wineskins can no longer contain what the Spirit is doing next.

For more than two decades I've had the honor of leading OneHope, a global ministry devoted to God's mission of engaging every child and young person with His Word. Along the way I've witnessed sweeping transformation, from the early days of print-based ministry to the frontiers of digital innovation, from grassroots outreach to global partnerships that have helped engage more than two billion young people with Scripture across every continent. I haven't merely observed disruption from a distance; I've walked through it. I've seen up close how each seismic shift in culture, technology, and communication has reshaped the way the next generation engages with Scripture.

And in every case, I've seen the same pattern: God uses seasons of upheaval to birth something new and powerful. He does more than just renew the Church—He reshapes entire cultures for His glory.

We are in such a moment now, and Dr. Terry Parkman understands this better than most.

Terry isn't just asking the hard questions; he's living in the tension of them daily. He has been on the front lines of generational ministry, wrestling with the practical realities of reaching Generations Z and Alpha. As a pastor and a voice to the next generation, he has spent years sitting with Gen Z and Gen Alpha, not as a critic of their culture but as a cultivator of their calling.

In *Future Church*, Terry doesn't offer simple answers or quick fixes. Instead, he provides what the Church desperately needs: a thoughtful, biblical framework for understanding the shifts happening around us and within us.

Having spent my life studying the moves of God across cultures and generations, I can tell you that every great awakening in history has required the Church to adapt its methods without compromising its message. The early Church moved from synagogues to homes. The Protestant Reformation leveraged the printing press. The modern missions movement embraced steamships and telegraph lines. Today, we face disruptions that dwarf all these: artificial intelligence, virtual reality, and cultural paradigm shifts that are reshaping how an entire generation thinks, learns, and relates.

Some see these changes as threats. Terry sees them as opportunities.

What you'll find in these pages is a vision of the Church that leans in to the future with faith instead of fear. This Church recognizes Generations Z and Alpha not as problems to solve but as God's chosen instruments to reach a rapidly changing world. Like Daniel in Babylon, they've been placed in a foreign culture—not to retreat from it but to transform it.

This message is timely. At OneHope, our global research has shown again and again that young people today are more spiritually open than we often assume, and they are more discerning than ever when it comes to authenticity. They can spot performance from a mile away. What they're searching for is truth wrapped in humility, from mentors who will walk with them and not just preach at them.

*Future Church* rises to that challenge. It equips us to lead through the rapid changes we're experiencing by inviting readers to think theologically and lead practically. It casts vision without losing touch with the day-to-day realities of ministry.

What I appreciate most is that this book never loses sight of the unchanging truth at the center of it all: Jesus Christ is the same yesterday, today, and forever. Our methods may evolve, but our message remains. The Gospel still transforms. The Spirit still leads. And the Church still has a future if we're willing to follow where He's going next.

As you read this book, you'll be challenged to think differently about discipleship, leadership, and mission. You'll discover practical insights for engaging digital natives without sacrificing spiritual depth. You'll gain clarity on how to navigate technological disruption without compromising biblical fidelity.

—Rob Hoskins, DMin
Cofounder and President, OneHope

# Letter to the Reader

Dear Reader,

This book you're holding is more than just words on paper—it's truly a labor of love. It represents over twenty years of my journey ministering to the next generation around the globe and more than a decade of diving deep into research across six continents. In all this I've been driven by a passion to understand the massive generational shifts, the cultural disruptions, and the incredible global connectedness brought about by new technologies. What I discovered reshaped not just how I see ministry but also my understanding of leadership and the future of the Church.

I felt compelled to write this book because I genuinely believe the Church is at a pivotal crossroads. We're moving into a future marked by rapid technological changes, cultural shifts, and generational transitions. And if we're going to thrive, the Church needs to be apostolic—boldly pioneering new paths and raising leaders who aren't just comfortable with disruption but actually thrive in it.

One passage from Scripture deeply motivates me: Judges 2:10, which talks about a generation rising up that "knew neither the Lord nor what He had done for Israel." That verse has always hit home for me, and I honestly don't want something like that happening on our watch or the watch of the generations we're raising up now.

As I travel and speak around the world, people often ask, "Terry, what should I read to understand the world like you do or think how you think?" Rather than sending them a bunch of different resources, I wanted to create one book that would serve as a foundational resource. My hope is that it highlights the critical trends shaping the next generation, helping you make intentional moves that you can pass along to others, sparking fresh ways of leading and discipling in our rapidly changing world.

Now, to be clear, this book doesn't claim to have all the answers. Think of it instead as a starting point, the beginning of a conversation I hope will continue long after you've turned the last page. Like the "sons of Issachar" in 1 Chronicles 12:32, I truly believe we have an incredible opportunity—and responsibility—to "understand the signs of the times and know the best course to take."

My prayer is that this book encourages and inspires you to courageously lead the Church into its exciting and promising future.

Let's pioneer together,

Terry

# Introduction

The Future Church isn't an institution to be preserved—it's a movement and a mission waiting to be mobilized.

We stand at a threshold moment. The speed of change—technological, cultural, generational—is more than fast; it's disruptive. Everything is accelerating, compounding, and breaking paradigms that held steady for decades. But this isn't something to fear. It's something to discern. It's something to steward.

Disruption is the language of this generation, and it just might be God's preferred language for this moment in history. From Genesis to Revelation, God uses disruption to shake the status quo and make way for something new. The cross disrupted the power of death. Pentecost disrupted the way faith was practiced. And today, I believe God is once again using disruption—not to threaten the Church but to propel it.

This book is for those who know we can't keep doing what we've always done and expect to reach a world that's already moved on. It's for pastors, pioneers, entrepreneurs, creatives, cultural translators, and anyone else who understands that while the Church's message is eternal, its methods must be elastic. The emerging generations—Z, Alpha, and soon Beta—aren't just the "next wave." They are already reshaping culture, technology, and spiritual hunger in ways that demand a response. They are globally connected, natively digital, and wired for rapid adaptation. But make no mistake, they are also spiritually open. In fact, many of them are searching for Jesus. The question isn't whether they're interested. It's whether we're speaking their language.

May I share a hard truth? Much of the Church is still calibrated for a world that no longer exists. We're offering analog ministry in a digital age. We're leaning on industrial models in an adaptive world. But instead of a death sentence, this is an invitation. In these pages we'll explore the four major ages that have shaped how humans understand identity and purpose—from the Agricultural Age to the Adaptive Age. We'll unpack the traits, challenges, and massive opportunities present within Gen Z and Alpha. We'll confront what it means to disciple people in the age of AI, Web3, and the metaverse—not with fear but with holy strategy. And we'll ask one of the most urgent questions facing the Church today: Will we ride the waves of disruption or get crushed by them?

My aim isn't to deconstruct. I'm not here to criticize the Church. I still believe in it. But I also believe it's time to change how we think about what comes next. It's time to build—not because God is different but because the world is.

If you've ever sensed that the models we inherited don't quite fit the mission ahead, if you've ever felt the tension between your theology and your tools, if you're convinced the Church's best days aren't behind us but right in front of us, this book is for you.

The Gospel is still good. Jesus still saves. The Church is still God's plan. But we—the body of Christ—must evolve. We always have. That's how revival works. So let's talk about what's happening. Let's wrestle with what's coming. And let's reimagine how the Church can rise—not in spite of disruption but because of it.

The future isn't something we need to fear. It's something we're called to lead.

# PART I

# WHERE WE HAVE BEEN

CHAPTER 1

# The Edge of Opportunity

If you are anything like me, you want to know the why of something before you commit to it. Whether watching the trailer before renting a movie on Amazon or researching a company before accepting a job interview, the goal is the same: You want knowledge to inform your judgment. In order to provide that for you in this book, I will begin with a short but true story. Afterward we will briefly unpack it.

In 2018 I had the opportunity to be with pastors who lead youth and young adult ministries from every nation in the Asia-Pacific region. We gathered in Bangkok, Thailand, for a summit to discuss what was impacting the next generation globally and to identify the changes we needed to make. What could we do as NextGen leaders to better engage and reach younger generations with the message of Jesus?

My topic centered on the impact of technology and how it has created a shift in what the next generation expects from the Church.

As I spoke passionately about this shift, something powerful took place that will forever mark my life. One national youth director for his denomination raised his hand to make a statement. Through his English translator he said, "Terry, based on what you're unpacking here, I can see where our young people are headed in the next ten years. We've never had an opportunity to really analyze where our youth are headed over a decade. I'm really excited because what you're teaching is helping us to see around the corner and prepare to meet the needs of the next generation in our nation."

After expressing my excitement, I noticed that another national youth director was weeping. I asked him what was wrong, and he composed himself and said, "Terry, ten years ago we started to notice how the same global shifts were impacting our young people in Japan. Because of their addiction to their screens, they have gone from being socially awkward to socially averse. When we approached our national leadership and asked if we could make changes within our ministries to meet these needs, we were told not to change a thing. In essence, we were told that by even suggesting that a change needed to be made, we were also saying that the way our predecessors structured the ministry is no longer sufficient."

He went on to say, "Ten years ago we had 30 teenagers, on average, in every church, and today we have an average of 0.7 teenagers in every church. If we had made the necessary changes then, we wouldn't have lost a generation today."

## AN UNSTOPPABLE FORCE

While the latter national youth director's account is tragic, it is also a cautionary tale for all of us who care deeply about the spiritual welfare of the next generation. And there is much hope.

As a researcher and pastor who has spent more than two decades focused on the beliefs and values of Generation Z (born 1997–2012), Generation Alpha (born 2013–2024), and now Generation Beta (beginning in 2025), I am fully convinced that we are living in an exceptional moment in history. Today more than ever, the Gospel can reach the ends of the earth in ways we previously only ever dreamed of.

God's Church—the collective body of Christ followers around the world—cannot be stopped, silenced, or sidelined, regardless of whatever disruptions come its way. I love the Church and have committed my life to it, but there is always room for change, especially when the world is shifting around us. While the message of the Gospel is unchanging, the methods we use to share it must change. We must constantly be vigilant in assessing and adapting the tools we use to reach each generation.

**While the message of the Gospel is unchanging, the methods we use to share it must change.**

These are two critical distinctions regarding the Church's future:

1] The message is alive and well, unchanging and indestructible. Jesus sums it up when He tells Peter that "on this rock I will build my church, and the gates of hell shall not prevail against it" (Matthew 16:18, ESV).

2] Due to the speed of change—cultural, societal, and technological—the thinking processes of our younger generations are radically different from those born before the advent of the internet (early 1990s). The next generation is connected and culturally savvy, and it has a native familiarity with disruption. When it comes to the fulfillment of the Great Commission, this is just the type of generation the Church has been praying for—agile, flexible, and adept at processing rapid change.

While we can fully place our hope in the Gospel and know with certainty that the Church is an unstoppable force, we face some steep challenges in this age. It's about form and function—the message *and* our methods of conveying it. Simply put, we embrace the fact that the message of Christ never changes, while the methods by which we engage our culture must.

If I had to choose one word to sum up what is happening right now to the Church and its ability to reach the burgeoning generations, it would be *disruption*. Here's *Merriam-Webster's* definition of the verb *disrupt*:

**1a:** to break apart**:** RUPTURE
**b:** to throw into disorder
**2a:** to interrupt the normal course or unity of
**b: (business:** to cause upheaval in (an industry, market, etc.)

As we will discuss in depth, disruption is a two-edged sword. On one hand, it can bring chaos (e.g., when the power grid crashes during a blackout) and calamity (e.g., the devastating disruption caused by a Category 5 hurricane).

On the other hand, disruption can also spur innovation and progress. When Henry Ford disrupted the transportation industry in 1908 with the mass production of the Model T, many criticized him for jeopardizing the future of horse travel and the railroad industry. (All three are alive and well, of course, nearly 120 years later.)

Likewise, I'm old enough to remember how Blockbuster failed to take Netflix seriously as a competitive threat. After all, how could a virtual video store that mailed DVDs to customers compete with neighborhood Blockbusters, where customers could rent videos and watch them the same day? But Blockbuster failed to anticipate the increasing speed of digital technology and Netflix's ability to deliver entertainment directly into customers' homes via ever-improving streaming services.

Netflix adapted; Blockbuster did not. Today, few people even recall that Netflix started as an entertainment mail-delivery service. Add to that the fact that the COVID-19 pandemic forced everyone to hunker down at home, causing even more disruption in the entertainment-delivery industry and the rapid expansion of streaming services worldwide.

In both cases—the mass production of the automobile and the advent of in-home entertainment streaming—disruption led to greater innovation and adaptation.

So how does disruption relate to the current state of the Church and its ability—or lack thereof—to engage, evangelize, and disciple those under the age of thirty? The Church needs to allow its methods to form around disruption without diluting the Gospel. In the case of my opening story, Asian NextGen leaders were lamenting the fact that just the opposite was happening for them: Their national leaders were resisting disruption and insisting that the younger leaders employ old (i.e., outdated) methods for the delivery of the Gospel.

However, the Gospel is fluid and takes the shape of any container it fills. The shape may change, but the contents remain pure. This is Missiology 101. As disruptions take place, the Church should allow form to change while function remains the same so that we may "become all things to all people so that by all means possible [we] might save some" (1 Corinthians 9:22).

**The Gospel is fluid and takes the shape of any container it fills.**

I am not in any way concerned about the survival of the Church. The Word assures us that Satan will be cast down and defeated, though for now he continues to be a disruptor of the worst kind here on Earth. However, God has always used disruption as a means of spreading the message. In fact, He is the original Disruptor, as shown through the Flood, the Exile, the Crucifixion, and Pentecost. God will continue to use disruption to shake up the status quo, advance His plans on Earth, and deploy His Church as an instrument to bring people into redemption and reconciliation with the Father.

In an unprecedented convergence of globalization, technology, and collective knowledge, Generations Z and Alpha emerge as the first truly global generations, speaking a digital language unseen since the era of Babel, poised at the precipice of either fulfilling the Great Commission or descending into spiritual apathy in a posttruth world.

In the following chapters we will delve into the heart of these pivotal generations, exploring how they are uniquely equipped to shape and navigate an ever-evolving world through emerging trends like Web3, the metaverse, and AI.

My purpose is not to focus on what's going wrong with the Church but rather to embark on an optimistic exploration of how these young, vibrant voices can lead societal transformation, embodying the change and hope that centuries of prayers have anticipated.

For those of us engaged in the work of God's Kingdom, disruption is a phenomenon to be understood and harnessed for His purposes. One of my goals is to shine a light on the power of disruption in the hands of a loving God by showing how the Church can embrace the current waves of technological, cultural, and societal disruptors crashing against its walls. As we better understand these disruptions and learn to use them to our Kingdom advantage, we can ride these waves of change rather than drown beneath them.

A key question emerges: Will the Church be able to successfully navigate the disruptions currently affecting society and culture (i.e., AI innovations, Web3, the metaverse, and other emerging digital technologies), or will it remain stuck in old paradigms and structures that fail to capture the hearts and minds of Generations Z, Alpha, and Beta?

We will grapple with this question throughout these pages, with the aim of finding an answer that positions the Church for the future. We will examine the sometimes overwhelming and rapidly evolving societal landscape in which we live, peeking around the corner at what lies ahead five, fifteen, and even twenty-five years from now.

We know the younger generations' *real need*: to know Jesus and make Him known. But do we truly understand their *felt needs*? What will bring them through the front door of your church? What are the best practices to keep them engaged once they're there? What does discipleship look like—not twenty or thirty years ago, when we lived in a culture that believed in absolute truth, but today, when truth is considered relative and subject to one's own experiences?

We live in a posttruth world, where emotion and opinion often trump absolutes and facts. How do we—those of us raised with clearly defined lines of right and wrong—adapt our methods to engage a generation where truth is fluid, personal, and rapidly changing? Again, we worship an unchanging God whose very name means truth. The challenge is presenting that truth in a "language" (i.e., method or set of methods) spoken by the next generation.

Though we cannot predict with full certainty what the Church will look like in fifteen or twenty years, I believe there are markers we can study to prepare ourselves so that God can use us in the midst of massive disruption. In my full-time work in NextGen ministry, I've been blessed to travel around the world and connect with like-minded Christians who share a passion for seeing the next generations reached for Jesus—not *in spite of* the digital and technological age in which we live but *in the midst of* it. Together we are using it, embracing it, and engaging it for Kingdom gains.

When we talk about reaching the next generation, we must understand that there need to be people who help translate culture for them. The Word of God frames this mandate brilliantly:

> From the tribe of Issachar, there were 200 leaders of the tribe with their relatives. All these men understood the signs of the times and knew the best course for Israel to take.
>
> —1 Chronicles 12:32, NLT

Believe me when I say that God does not leave a generation without its own tribe of Issachar. He appoints a remnant that understands "the signs of the times" and helps the Church discern the direction it should go. And by and large, the tribe of Issachar in each generation is composed of people who lead the next generation.

Those who have become students of the younger culture have devoted time and effort to speaking to a digital age in terms it can relate to. We are members of that tribe of Issachar, helping the Church know the direction it should go by reading the signs of the times—by exegeting and discerning culture and helping people understand and translate it.

Arguably, humankind has not experienced such an intense period of disruption since the time of Babel, when all the people of the earth spoke one common language. Today, like then, our younger generations "speak" one language—a digital, technological language with its own grammar, dialects, subcultures, and ways of interacting that transcend national borders and ideologies.

Our job is to understand this language so we can understand the people who speak it—which is exactly what Jesus modeled. Think about how Jesus met people where they were—in the taverns, on the roads, in the cities, and in the synagogues. When He approached the unapproachable Zacchaeus sitting in that tree, Jesus already knew the tax collector's greatest needs—and He met them.[1] When Jesus arrived at Jacob's well and asked the Samaritan woman to draw water for Him, He knew it was an "unclean" act, but He did it anyway.[2] Why? To disrupt the oppressive cultural and religious structures that hindered His mission of reconciliation and to break through them with the love of God.

Jesus constantly went to great lengths to reach people right where they were in order to lead them to where He wanted them to be. Sometimes a good shaking was needed. Could Jesus have healed Lazarus from afar? Yes, but He chose to raise him from the dead four days later instead. Martha even pointed out, "The smell will be terrible" (John 11:39, NLT). *Disruption.* Entering into an area filled with pigs—the epitome of an unclean environment—to heal a tormented demoniac?[3] *Disruption.* Healing the servant of a faith-filled Roman "enemy" with just a word? And even more, Jesus proclaims, "I tell you, not even in Israel have I found such faith" (Luke 7:9, ESV). Major *disruption.*

Disruption is here—now, today, and in full force. The question for God's Church isn't, "How can we defeat or sidestep disruption?" Rather, the question is, "How does God want to use this particular kind of disruption—technological, cultural, societal—to reach more people with the Gospel?"

■ ■

**Disruption is here—now, today, and in full force.**

■ ■

Will the Church resist the waves of change, or will it ride those waves to reach more people in even the most resistant and diverse areas of the world?

Will we—the sons and daughters of Issachar—rise to the challenge God sets before us?

I believe the answer is a resounding yes—*if* we are willing to invest the time and effort to listen, learn, and embrace new ways of translating and articulating His eternal message. I believe God's Church—His body of believers the world over—is on the edge of an unprecedented opportunity to help raise a new generation of Jesus followers who think, connect, and interact in radically different ways than most of us over the age of forty. They are the emerging tribe of Issachar: They understand the times, speak the language of their culture, and are ready to be equipped to reach their peers worldwide.

It is, indeed, an exciting time for the future of the Church.

## CHAPTER 2

# The Three Paradigm Shifts

*Whoever has ears, let them hear what the Spirit says to the churches.*
—Revelation 2:29

Understanding the beliefs, values, and felt needs of any generation is important for those of us who have a deep interest in reaching that generation for Christ. But to fully explore the beliefs and values of younger generations, it's important to first define our terms. For our purposes, here is a breakdown of the generations since the turn of the twentieth century:

- **The Greatest Generation:** Born c. 1901–1924
- **The Silent Generation:** Born c. 1925–1945
- **Baby Boomers:** Born c. 1946–1964

- **Generation X:** Born c. 1965–1980
- **Millennials:** Born c. 1981–1996
- **Generation Z:** Born c. 1997–2012
- **Generation Alpha:** Born c. 2013–2025
- **Generation Beta:** Born c. 2025–2039

While some experts use different terms or groupings (e.g., some refer to the Silent Generation as the Baby Builders), these designations serve our purposes and provide a plumb line for reference.

As I write this in spring 2025, we are on the brink of the oldest Boomers turning eighty, and the oldest Millennials turning forty-five. This means the rising leaders in the Church are the younger Millennials and older members of Generation Z—and right around the corner are Generations Alpha and Beta.

Without question this swath of Americans—those born in the late 1990s through today—is coming of age in the most technologically advanced sliver of time in human history. They have grown up with the explosion of the internet, the proliferation of the personal computer, and the ubiquity of the smartphone. Now, as they assume leadership positions in business and technology, they face a world where the speed at which trends and cycles change is increasing at a dizzying rate.

What's the key word for survival in this Digital Age of frenetic change?

*Adaptation.*

One of the most radical periods of cultural adaptation occurred in just the past sixty or so years. Social anthropologist Margaret Mead foresaw this major change on the horizon in the second half of the twentieth century. The following is my own summary of her ideas from *Culture and Commitment: A Study of the Generation Gap*:

> Throughout history, most cultures have been postfigurative, where parents and grandparents help young to understand future.

> A few times it becomes cofigurative where change happens so fast that society depends on young to help understand the future. Mead anticipated a time coming in history where technology changes so fast that culture, for the first time in human history, will be prefigurative where the children will have to figure out for themselves what their values will be.[4]

Mead captured this societal upheaval by describing the way each generation learns and processes culture:

1] **Postfigurative**—For the vast majority of time humans have walked the earth, cultures across the globe have been past oriented, with a strong emphasis on one's elders and ancestors. The *modus operandi* was to educate, inform, and raise the present generation based on the morals, myths, and methods passed down by former generations. (This is still the case today in some parts of developing countries and in cultures that continue to revere their elders.)

2] **Cofigurative**—In a cofigurative culture things are present focused, and cultural values and beliefs are formed among others in the same generation. Culture is formed and informed, then, through peer-to-peer interaction, rather than through a person's elders or ancestors. Mead pointed to the youth movements of the 1960s and 1970s as an example of cofigurative culture, which she believed arose because of the collapse of postfigurative society—especially in developed nations.

3] **Prefigurative**—In a prefigurative culture the emphasis is future focused and knowledge is transmitted from the youth to the elders. Mead said, "I call this new style prefigurative because in this new culture it will be the child—and not the parent and grandparent—that represents what is to come."[5] For

> the first time in human history, youth know more about the world than their parents or grandparents. With the advent of the computer and other modern technologies, Mead predicted that rapid acceleration in the way we learn and interact would bring about this unprecedented shift. And half a century later her predictions are coming true.

As the Church, it's critical for us to understand that this current generation does not think, learn, or interact with the world in the same way most of us did (especially if you—like me—were born before 1990, when the Information Age began to accelerate rapidly). The vast majority of American adults over thirty-five were raised in a postfigurative world.

In light of this prefigurative cultural phenomenon, we can no longer depend on postfigurative ways of thinking and teaching. For example, have you been to an Apple store lately? In Apple's training workshops you will mostly find employees under thirty-five teaching those older than them how to effectively operate their iPhones, iPads, and MacBooks. This is one example of prefigurative learners teaching cofigurative parents (like me). But even more, prefigurative learners teach one another—rather than turning to their parents or grandparents.

Again, the key word here is *adaptation*. How can God's Church adapt to this bold new prefigurative world in ways that glorify Jesus and engage the maximum number of hearts and minds?

I don't believe it's a stretch to say that we can apply the phrase *radical adaptation* to what's been happening to the Church in the US over the past several decades. While I do not believe the Church in America is dying, I do believe it is struggling to adapt to radical cultural and technological changes. I'm not saying we need to embrace radical cultural trends; rather, we need to understand how to adapt our local church models to meet the needs of the people who fill our churches.

Take, for example, the decrease in the number of Americans who (1) are religiously affiliated or (2) define themselves as committed Christians. The Public Religion Research Institute (PRRI) reported the following statistics on those who claim to be religiously unaffiliated (i.e., not part of any denomination or religious movement):

- 34 percent of Generation Z
- 35 percent of Millennials
- 25 percent of Generation X
- 19 percent of Baby Boomers
- 15 percent of the Silent Generation[6]

Not surprisingly, age also plays a large part in whether a person identifies as Christian. Here are the breakdowns by age group as of 2022, showing the percentage of people in each group who identify as Christian:

- 55 percent of those ages 18–29
- 62 percent of those ages 30–49
- 74 percent of those ages 50–64
- 77 percent of those age 65 and over[7]

What these studies—and many others—reveal is an eye-opening US trend: Generations Z and Alpha are increasingly unaffiliated when it comes to religion. In fact, the Pew Research Center estimates that by 2070 the "nones" (those who answer "none" when asked about religious background or affiliation) could constitute more than half of all American adults.[8] Never before in our nation's history have the religiously unaffiliated outnumbered those who claim Christianity as their religion of choice.

**We need to understand how to adapt our local church models to meet the needs of the people who fill our churches.**

Recent data, however, reveals an intriguing story with a silver lining. According to the Religious Landscape Study (RLS) by Pew Research, the long-term decline in the number of Americans who identify as Christian is slowing significantly. In the first RLS (2007), 78 percent of US adults identified as Christian. That number fell to 71 percent in 2014 and now stands at 62 percent (as of RLS 2023–2024). While the overall trend still reflects a downward trajectory, Pew notes that from 2019–2024 the percentage of US adults identifying as Christian has held fairly steady, ranging from 60–64 percent.[9]

And the news gets better:

> According to Barna's latest data, 66 percent of all U.S. adults say they have made a personal commitment to Jesus that is still important in their life today. That marks a 12-percentage-point increase since 2021, when commitment levels reached their lowest in more than three decades of Barna tracking.[10]

We will study this statistic at length in chapter 6.

*The Open Generation: United States* project conducted in 2021 by Barna Group and its partners found that teens (13–17) are very open to Jesus. For example, when asked, "Throughout the rest of your life, how motivated are you to continue learning more about Jesus Christ?" an encouraging 77 percent of all teens said they were either very motivated (52 percent) or somewhat motivated (25 percent) to get to know Him better.[11]

When false rumors circulated about his death, Mark Twain quipped, "The report of my death was an exaggeration." Similarly, Barna Group CEO David Kinnaman said, "The rumors of Christianity's demise among younger people are greatly exaggerated. . . . That's, I think, a really important story."[12]

And I agree—it is a very important story. I believe the previous information tells us two things:

1] The Church is struggling to attract Generations Z and Alpha as affiliates (consistent attendees, members, etc.).
2] There is a keen interest in Jesus among the younger generations.

I don't believe those two statements are contradictory. A person can be hesitant to join an organized denomination or movement but still have a strong desire to know more about Jesus. We do ourselves a disservice when we view this trend through an Information Age lens that equates church attendance with spiritual commitment. Instead, we must regard Generation Z's reticence with sober realism and acknowledge, "They are not responding to our church model, so we must adapt the model."

**There is a keen interest in Jesus among the younger generations.**

The data suggests that those under thirty want Jesus, but they don't necessarily want to engage with Him in existing or traditional ways. The tables have turned. As someone who rides the line between Gen X and Millennial (Xennial), I remember when statistics showed that eight out of ten young people would say no to being invited to church, and if not church, then hearing another person's story of how Jesus transformed their life.

Today, six out of ten teens are open to hearing more about Jesus. The big question we need to ask is whether our churches are built and equipped to reach a generation that no longer fills the pews. Put another way, How can we adapt our postfigurative ways of doing church to better engage a prefigurative culture? Do we have evangelism strategies that reflect a resistant generation when instead we should be building evangelism models to reach, as Barna Group calls it, an Open Generation?

That's a conundrum for the Church—a big adaptation challenge that will not be convenient, easy, or cheap. But make no mistake, radical changes are on our doorstep. It's time for the Church to embrace the qualities Jesus modeled, such as compassion for those different from us, a willingness to meet people exactly where they are, and an unflinching, unwavering commitment to the eternal truths of God's Word and His Kingdom.

The pressing question, then, is not whether the next generation is open to learning more about Jesus. Rather, what are the most effective and efficient ways to engage the younger generations with the message of Christ? Before we attempt to answer, it's important to gain a bit more context. In our commitment to win these younger generations to Christ, we must learn what makes them tick—their values, belief systems, and the culture in which they are coming of age. We must be willing to consider and question the presuppositions we were raised on in the Church—not the message itself but the methods by which the message was taught to us. That's where adaptation becomes critical.

In the next chapter I want to take a bird's-eye view of the four major cultural and societal paradigms throughout human history: the Agricultural, Industrial, Information, and Adaptive Ages. My goal is to provide context for where we came from, where we are now, and where I believe we are headed.

# CHAPTER 3

# The Four Ages of History

For each age of history major disruptions and adaptive skills were (and are) needed by the respective cultures most affected. And in each age God's message never changes. Faithful men and women of the Way—a remnant—have been able to recognize the disruptions and adapt with radical new techniques and methods.

As the Church, it's critical that we understand not only where we have come from—culturally and as a society—but also where we are now and where we are headed. Knowledge is power, as the saying goes, and when we combine this knowledge with our desire to disciple the nations, God can use the youth of today to empower the Church of tomorrow.

**God can use the youth of today to empower the Church of tomorrow.**

With that larger framework of "How should the Church live now?" in this chaotic, confusing world, I want to explore the four major cultural and societal ages that have brought us to where we are today. In so doing, my goal is to provide context for how the Church can best serve and raise up the younger generations.

## AGRICULTURAL AGE (ADAM–1750): VALUED FOR WHO YOU ARE

As believers in Christ, we embrace the biblical understanding that who we are is not based on temporal or worldly metrics but on the truth that we are children of God who have been gifted eternal life through Jesus' sacrifice. We are, indeed, made in the image of God—the *imago Dei*—and nothing can change that. But the truth of our identity in Christ has not always been reflected in the times in which our ancestors lived. Societal structures—such as who you are in terms of bloodlines—have often run contrary to the Gospel message that in Christ "there is neither Jew nor Gentile, neither slave nor free, nor is there male and female, for you are all one in Christ Jesus" (Galatians 3:28).

For the first several eras of humanity's existence, who your father and mother were had a great deal to do with who you were in the strata of society. This was a key hallmark of the Agricultural Age, during which the vast majority lived an agrarian lifestyle. Beginning, arguably, in the Fertile Crescent, nestled between the Euphrates and Tigris Rivers of modern-day Iraq, humanity transitioned from a hunter-gatherer existence to one of cultivation.

Amazingly, that's the way things remained until just the last 250 or so years. People rarely traveled more than twenty miles from their birthplace. That's where they were born and raised, where they married, and where they had children and grandchildren. And that's where they died—either in or near their ancestral home. The land was mostly untamed, and people competed with nature to survive. Most people were poor, and the wealthy few ruled and led them. The middle class was small or nonexistent, depending on the culture.

In the Agricultural Age identity was deeply rooted in community, family, and religious tradition. The critical question was, "Who are you?" In this period an individual's worth was tied to their identity within the natural order and their role within the community. Later in this period the schoolhouse was often the same building as the church, and the most educated person in the room was often the parson or the pastor. Royalty and the religious leaders could read—most others could not.

Think about it this way: If your family immigrated from another country during this time, chances are they found land and built a generational home where multiple generations could thrive. You were known by your last name. Telling people who you were gave them a glimpse into your generational history.

Ancient Rome provides another example of the importance of lineage. If you were born into slavery in ancient Rome, you were likely to live out your days as a slave—along with your children and their children. And in medieval societies, if you were born a serf (one who works the land in exchange for the right to live on that same land), chances were you would remain a serf, as would your children and their children.

Conversely, if you were born into Roman aristocracy—patrician society based on elite bloodlines—you were virtually guaranteed a life of entitlement and privilege. The same could be said of the upper classes in feudal England, where lords ruled (and stayed wealthy), and vassals worked and paid taxes (and remained poor). For centuries, this was the cultural norm. Who you were was determined by who your parents were in terms of class status, bloodlines, and titles.

It's hard to believe that just 125 years ago the majority of people still lived outside urban—and suburban—centers. If your grandfather was born before 1950, he most likely sat on the knee of *his* grandfather and heard stories about growing up in the country and working the land. In fact, the 1920 US Census reported for the first time that the number of Americans living in urban areas outnumbered those living in rural areas.[13]

Even though the Agricultural Age officially ended some 150 years earlier, the rural lifestyle was still predominant into the early part of the twentieth century. The shadow cast by the Agricultural Age loomed over your great-grandparents, your grandparents, and perhaps even your own parents, particularly if they lived in a rural area. In other words, Boomers are old enough to have heard firsthand stories from the last generations to live primarily outside the city. As we engage with the younger generations, it's important to keep this in mind: Our frame of reference as Boomers or Gen Xers is very different from theirs, influenced possibly by our ancestors' memories of the Agricultural Age and most definitely by the Industrial and Information Ages.

## INDUSTRIAL AGE (1750–1950): VALUED FOR WHAT YOU DO

Beginning in England in the mid-eighteenth century, industrialization and the mass production of goods began to transform Western societies. With inventions like the assembly line, steam engine, telegraph, and spinning jenny (which allowed a single worker to spin multiple threads of yarn simultaneously), a genuine revolution was under way—one that would usher in a radically new paradigm for living daily life.

For the first time ever, the mass production of food made it possible for more people to leave their family farms and seek better-paying work in the cities. As food became more readily available, daily life was no longer based on nutritional subsistence (i.e., the need to focus on feeding one's family *each day*). This allowed mobility and the possibility of finding work in an urban factory, office, or shop.

Slowly but surely, Europe and the US transitioned from agrarian societies to urban societies. This changed everything, from the workday to the educational system to the economy as a whole. By the early twentieth century, and for the first time in human history, more people lived in cities than in the countryside.

The Industrial Age shifted value from identity (who you are) to function, asking, "What do you do?" People were ascribed value based on what they did for a living as opposed to who their ancestors were. A middle class began to rise, whereas in the Agricultural Age, it had been minuscule. As the middle class grew, so did this value shift from "Who are your parents?" to "What can you do?"

In the Industrial Age, with the move from agrarian to urban living, society began to think like consumers rather than cultivators (e.g., farmers). No longer did a growing majority of people need to produce a living from the earth; rather, they worked in factory and manufacturing jobs to enable them to consume. Livelihood came from a paycheck rather than a plow.

With this in mind, *production*, *performance*, and *quantity* were highly valued during this age. One was promoted or esteemed based on the laws of the assembly line: *What are you producing? How well do you perform? How much product do you turn out by the end of your shift?* Do these three things well in the Industrial Age, and you had it made.

Another significant development during that time was the birth of consumerism. Goods such as textiles, food, household items, hardware, and furniture became much more readily available due to industrial and manufacturing advancements. Instead of making their clothing, growing their food, and building their homes and furnishings, many people were able to obtain these items affordably in the marketplace and on Main Street.

## INFORMATION AGE (1950–2022): VALUED FOR WHAT YOU THINK

Around 1950 the Industrial Age was transitioning to the Information Age. The first great invention of the Information Age was the transistor in 1947, which allowed for the rapid development of information processing. By the early 1970s the invention of microprocessors, combined with improvements in mainframe technology, began to miniaturize computers as the Information Age gained speed and momentum. And though technological advancements allowed for better information processing speeds and quality, few could predict what would come next—an invention that would forever alter the world and the way we communicate.

On a classic 70-degree fall day in Los Angeles in1969, history was made: "A team of students led by Leonard Kleinrock, distinguished professor of computer science at the UCLA Samueli School of Engineering, sent the first message over the ARPANET."[14] That message traveled over the early computer network to colleagues at the Stanford Research Institute in Palo Alto, California, some 350 miles away.

According to Kleinrock, they intended to transmit the word "LOGIN," but the system crashed after they had sent the first two letters. Kleinrock writes, "So, the very first message on the Internet was the prescient word 'lo' (as in, 'lo and behold!'). We hadn't prepared a special message (as did, for example, Samuel Morse with 'What Hath God Wrought') but our 'lo' could not have been a more succinct, a more powerful or a more prophetic message." [15]

The first "node"—or connection point—of the internet became room 3420 in Boelter Hall on the UCLA campus, and those two letters—the first of trillions of messages to come—were transmitted at 10:30 p.m. on October 29, 1969. Fast-forward twenty years, and the World Wide Web (www) was proposed in 1989, making it possible for ordinary people to access this powerful new communication tool called the internet.

The 1980s saw the advent of personal computing with the rise of Apple and Microsoft, which created a shift in economic power toward information technologies. It was the start of a widely recognized "post-industrial" or "information-based" society. In 1993 the World Wide Web was released into the public domain, and by 1995 the internet was available to everyone with a computer and a phone line in much of the developed world.[16]

The birth and growth of the internet irrevocably changed the way the world interacted and communicated. Not since the invention of the printing press in 1440 by Johannes Gutenberg has the world's method of communication been so dramatically altered.

**The birth and growth of the internet irrevocably changed the way the world interacted and communicated.**

The Information Age introduced a world where knowledge is power. Instead of "Who are you?" or "What do you do?" the questions of value became "What do you think?" and "How much do you know?" The rise of technology and instant access to information shifted the focus to intellectual capital. In this age what you learned in college over four years would launch a pattern of continual learning that would sustain you for the next four decades, and an increase in knowledge meant promotion.

The great paradigm shift from Agricultural Age cultivators to Industrial Age consumers forever altered the way we receive, process, and interpret information. Again, the key question changed from "Who are you?" (family, background, heritage) to "What do you do?" (lawyer, doctor, factory worker, machinist). This consumer-driven way of thinking dominated Western culture into and past the mid-twentieth century.

In the Information Age we moved from being consumers to publishers. Rather than internalizing the external (i.e., spectating and consuming), we began to engage with the world interactively via our devices, and our brains were rewired to externalize what we internalize (i.e., consume and publish). Rather than simply an information-in mentality, we took on a mindset that says, "Information *in* and processed, and then published content *out*." This shift was made possible by constantly clicking the "like" button, reposting, sharing, commenting, blogging, and vlogging. We have now become conditioned to publish everything we consume.

## ADAPTIVE AGE (2022–?): VALUED FOR HOW YOU MOVE

While we are still in the Information Age, we are transitioning into the next phase: the Adaptive Age. This new age is being shaped by three culture-shifting technological phenomena, all of which are considered adaptive technologies:

1] **Artificial intelligence (AI).** Though the building blocks for AI have been around for several decades, it wasn't until the last few years that AI became a household term and an ever-increasing presence in our daily lives. AI is here, and it is ubiquitous.
2] **Web3**. The next generation of the internet—dubbed Web3—will be decentralized, integrated, and a place where users have more control of their own data, identity, and destiny.
3] **The metaverse**. According to Mark Zuckerberg and his company, Meta: "The metaverse is the next evolution in social connection and the successor to the mobile internet. Like the internet, the metaverse will help you connect with people when you aren't physically in the same place and get us even closer to that feeling of being together in person."[17]

Many assumed that Generation Alpha, following Generation Z, would move from being consumers (Industrial Age) to publishers (Information Age) to creators (Web3/metaverse). However, the reality is that they are transitioning into *adapters* (Adaptive Age). This generation is growing up in a world where disruption is the norm—from micro-level shifts every few months to macro-level changes every six months. Theirs is the first generation to normalize AI/Web3 and constant change, making them native inhabitants of an adaptive world.

■ ■

**We have now become conditioned to publish everything we consume.**

■ ■

Consider the dramatic shift regarding vocation and today's job market. A recent ZipRecruiter survey found that 44 percent of job seekers regret their choice of degree because their education did not prepare them for the rapid changes in the workforce.[18] Even more startling is the World Economic Forum's *Future of Jobs* report, which predicts "65% of children entering primary school today will work in job categories that don't yet exist."[19] The upshot is that the half-life of skills (attained in school or on the job) is shrinking rapidly. What is learned today becomes obsolete in less than five years in many fields, especially in the technology sector. That means by the time someone graduates from college, their skills will face redundancy before mastery.

The shift into the Adaptive Age has been characterized by constant change, disruption, and the necessity for rapid adaptation. Today, the question isn't, "Who are you?" or, "What do you do?" or even, "What do you think?" but instead, "How do you adapt?" Success is no longer determined by what you know but by how quickly you can learn, adapt, and apply new skills. For Generation Alpha, who will live and work in a world reshaped by AI and digital disruption, the ability to adapt and move forward is essential. (We will explore these themes in the final chapter.)

To recap, over the past 275 years, the way we process the world has shifted in the following ways:

- **Agricultural Age:** Adam to approximately 1750 → "Who are you?" → *Cultivators*
- **Industrial Age:** 1750s–1950s → "What do you do?" → *Consumers*
- **Information Age:** 1950s–2022 → "What do you think?" → *Publishers*
- **Adaptive Age:** 2022–? → "How do you adapt?" → *Adapters*

## THE FUTURE CHURCH IN THE ADAPTIVE AGE

As we will discuss in chapter 8, the future of the Church depends on its ability to disciple these burgeoning generations—Z, Alpha, and Beta—in a way that is both contextually relevant and theologically grounded. The four ages—Agricultural, Industrial, Information, and Adaptive—offer a lens through which we can understand the changing nature of culture and discipleship.

■ ■

**The Church must prepare Generations Alpha and Beta to move with God in a world that is constantly shifting.**

■ ■

As we move deeper into the Adaptive Age, the Church must prepare Generations Alpha and Beta to move with God in a world that is constantly shifting. By grounding discipleship in the unchanging image of God and one's identity in Christ, the Church can position itself to successfully equip the next generations—not just to survive in the Adaptive Age but to thrive as transformative agents of God's Kingdom, bringing His truth, love, and justice to every corner of the world, digital or otherwise.

# PART II

# WHERE WE ARE

# CHAPTER 4

# Meet Generations Z and Alpha

***gen·er·a·tion** - je-nə-'rā-shən: a body of living beings constituting a single step in the line of descent from an ancestor*[20]

By the close of World War II, English was overtaking French as the world's *lingua franca*—the primary language used in diplomacy, business, science, technology, and aviation. English usage rose from approximately 405.7 million speakers in 1921 to more than 1.3 billion in 2021.[21] And more than 70 percent of those who now speak English are non-native speakers (i.e., English is not their first language).[22]

The rise of the English language during the Cold War paralleled the rise of technological advancements such as the microprocessor and computer miniaturization. In fact, by the time the internet started entering households in the mid-1990s, the stage was set for a major digital revolution.

As digital technologies improved, it became possible for the first time in history to communicate instantly—and cheaply—with anyone else in the world via a phone line and computer. It was the perfect environment for the rise of a new type of language—one that was digital, global, and pervasive.

Enter Generation Z (1997–2012), the first fully native internet generation. Whereas the vast majority of Millennials (1981–1996) were born before the internet became mainstream, every Gen Z baby was born during the normalization and dissemination period of the internet.

With Gen Z came a cultural barrier-shattering confluence of growing global English language proficiency and increasing ease of access to digital tools and rapid communication. Walls such as distance, technology, and language began crashing down all around the world. If a teen girl in Nairobi had internet access through her home or a local internet café, she could communicate in near real time with a teen girl in, say, New York, Cairo, Moscow, or Toronto.

Before the internet's explosion, that girl in Nairobi *could* have communicated with the teen in New York. She could have made a long-distance phone call (expensive), sent a fax (expensive and less available), or sent a letter (a wonderful means of communication but slow). But thanks to the internet, the barriers to real-time, affordable, and accessible communication were beginning to fall around the world.

The spread of the internet was like a digital tsunami whose influence radiated from the technological epicenters of the world—Silicon Valley, Tokyo, Bangalore, Shenzhen, and Tel Aviv—and swiftly made its way across oceans and continents. As of 2024 two-thirds of the world's population is online (that is, has access to the internet and uses it, even if infrequently).[23] Unsurprisingly, the younger a person is, the more likely they are to be online. But perhaps surprisingly, the generation gap is not very wide. In the US, for example, more than

99 percent of youth use the internet. That number drops slightly with age, as 90 percent of those 65 and older are online.[24]

Even more interesting is the staggering rate of assimilation driven by modern technological advancements. For context, consider the use of the telephone compared with that of the internet. Invented in 1876, the telephone took nearly forty-five years before just a third of American households had one (by 1920).[25] That number rose to 45 percent by 1945, 75 percent by 1957, and more than 90 percent by 1970.[26] In other words, it took nearly a century for the vast majority of Americans to become telephonic.

In contrast, it took less than thirty years for the internet, via the World Wide Web, to go from a novelty to a staple found in more than 90 percent of American homes. The significance of this cannot be overstated.

For millennia we had to work hard to communicate across distances. From the invention of the wheel to the first sailing vessel, from the horse stirrup to the steam engine, new devices slowly made the world a smaller, more accessible place. But every invention across all the millennia that came before pales in comparison to the internet. In just a single generation, everything has changed—the way we think, work, play, and connect. Enter the Digital Era, along with the first truly global generation: Gen Z.

## THE LANGUAGE OF GENERATION Z

If I had to pick one word to describe Generation Z, I believe a good contender would be *global*. By *global*, I'm not simply speaking geographically. I'm referring to the fact that Generations Z and Alpha are the first native generations with the ability to communicate and connect with virtually anyone, almost anywhere across the globe. By *global* I mean:

**They are speaking the same linguistic language.**

Generations Z and Alpha are capitalizing on the rise of English as the *lingua franca,* which allows youth from across the globe to converse. Put simply, not only are they digitally connected, but they also understand each other. Even more, with the translation tools of most search engines and social media apps, the communication barriers drop even further.

**Not only are they digitally connected, but they also understand each other.**

**They are speaking the same digital language.**

Youth are growing up with tools unheard of and foreign to even the last generation: AI, the metaverse, and Web3. With the envisioned decentralization of the internet—an internet not controlled or run by tech corporations but instead operated by blockchain technology—the new generations will be less influenced by the companies that now operate much of what is done online (e.g., Google, Microsoft, and Apple). Think many players on the Monopoly board with equal numbers of houses and hotels, rather than just two or three entities controlling the board.

**They are speaking the same cultural language.**

Back in the 1980s (when Baby Boomers were coming of age), television and films allowed icons such as Argentinean soccer great Maradona, NBA superstar Michael Jordan, and pop star Michael Jackson to become household names across the globe. In contrast, anyone today with a computer or smartphone can become an internet influencer with followers around the world. In other words, the digital era has leveled the playing field. Access brings opportunity.

Access has also brought like-minded thinking among young people experiencing the same types of trauma: the COVID-19 pandemic, the war in Ukraine (the largest conventional war in Europe since World War II), the killing of George Floyd and its aftermath, political divisiveness, and more.

They are also experiencing life in the posttruth era, where "likes" are often garnered by emotional responses rather than factual bases. Create the meme that hits hard regarding presidential elections, and emotions are triggered—the "likes" flood in. As the number of "likes" rises, social media algorithms adjust, and the same type of content pops up on the feeds of those with similar interests.

There's an old joke about Adlai Stevenson, a liberal who lost (twice) to Dwight D. Eisenhower for president in the 1950s. On a swanky street on the Upper East Side of Manhattan, one wealthy liberal said to his friend about Stevenson, "I don't understand. Everyone I know voted for him!" The point is that we tend to build our cultural tribe around others with the same values, opinions, and principles. The analogy still holds true today, but of course, it's much easier and faster to access one's tribe via the internet.

Today, however, in a posttruth society, emotions trump facts. Suddenly, an entire tribe of like-minded (or more accurately, like-emoted) folks is viewing similar kinds of material. Cultural clustering—or tribalism—is nothing new. For Generation X it was *Oprah*, *60 Minutes*, and *Good Morning America*. For Millennials it's Jimmy Fallon, X (formerly Twitter), Fox News, and MSNBC. For Generation Z it's TikTok, Instagram, YouTube, and a vast array of media personalities across those algorithm-driven worldwide platforms.

Going back to our Michael Jordan example of the '80s and '90s: You could walk the streets of Lagos or Tokyo and see his face plastered on T-shirts and on the sides of buses. But megastars like Jordan and tropes like *Baywatch* were where cultural commonalities ended between those kids in Japan and Nigeria. Today we have the new digital tribalism, whereby groups of like-minded people in the same demographic are gathering, sharing, clicking, and liking. It's now possible for that teen in Lagos to be online friends with the one in Tokyo.

It's also now possible for kids to buzz between "gardens" of content (Instagram, TikTok, online gaming, etc.) and then bring the "pollen" of those ideas with them to a new garden, where the content cross-pollinates and blooms. Of course, this leads to hives of like-minded people interacting, sharing, and liking similar types of pollen circulating within the garden.

It's a snowball effect on a scale we've never seen before: a generation of people with the ability to interact instantly with virtually anyone in the world, connect around common interests, and live a quarter (or even a third) of their lives in a virtual world increasingly disconnected from the physical one around them. It's no surprise when a fifty-something person "just doesn't get" the Super Bowl halftime show featuring the hottest Black rapper, while their sixteen-year-old son thinks he's "sending a powerful message" (literally something that happened in my home between my parents and me). Our society has always had culture gaps, but what is happening today is more like a culture gulf.

**Our society has always had culture gaps, but what is happening today is more like a culture gulf.**

This is due in part to the fact that the brains of the digitally native are being rewired online. Their virtual world is becoming their reality. They are collecting, processing, creating, and publishing content faster than we can imagine—faster than any generation before them. But what they are doing the most is adapting to the speed at which technology is evolving and in ways no other generation in US history has had to do.

**They are speaking the same prefigurative language.**

Recall our overview of the four ages of history the world has experienced since the beginning of human civilization: the Agricultural Age, the Industrial Age, the Information Age, and the Adaptive Age. Across the sweep of the millennia, we have gone from "Who are you?" (Agricultural Age), to "What do you do for a living?" (Industrial Age), to "What do you think?" (Information Age), and now to "How well can you adapt?" (Adaptive Age).

Next, let's overlay the ways cultures have acquired and disseminated learning and wisdom, one generation to the next. We have gone from wisdom and learning come from elders (past focused and postfigurative) to wisdom and learning are peer-to-peer (present focused and cofigurative), to wisdom and learning come from youth to elders (future focused and prefigurative).

As we discussed, in a prefigurative culture the emphasis is future focused, and knowledge is transmitted from youth to the elders. This is such an important phenomenon for the Church that it's worth breaking down further.

To put this in context, let's think about the way most of us over forty have attained the knowledge we needed to earn a living. After high school we either pursued a trade, entered the workforce in an entry-level position, or attended college or university. With all these pathways we were reminded—verbally and nonverbally—that the acquisition and mastery of our vocation's tools take time (many years, if not decades). And the common ascent up the corporate (or trade) ladder took time—we needed to wait our turn until our elders moved on or retired.

People over forty, such as me, think mostly with an Industrial-Information mix and frame of reference. We were trained by our elders and superiors, we have paid (or are paying) our dues, and we will eventually become the elder or superior. It is a vertical system where we start at the bottom (in our twenties and early thirties) and work our way upward.

But now? In a time when we are transitioning from Information to Adaptive thinking and living, everything is changing. The proverbial apple cart isn't just being turned over—it's being removed and replaced by an entirely new apple delivery system.

Enter the era of prefigurative thinking and living. It's a world where job skills, social trends, and even values and principles cycle through twice a year—and the process is speeding up. In this world natively inhabited by Generations Z and Alpha, the thinking or frame of reference isn't vertical—it's *horizontal*. The ladders of success are being dismantled and replaced by a network of horizontal pathways whereby the younger generations must learn *from one another*. Is it because they do not revere or respect their parents and elders? In most cases, no. It's because for the first time in history their parents don't have all the tools their children need to survive in this new world of technological complexity and adaptation.

**The thinking or frame of reference isn't vertical—it's *horizontal*.**

The One Laptop Per Child (OLPC) initiative, founded by faculty at MIT, underscored the profound potential of unconventional literacy efforts in developing nations. Writing for *Fast Company* in 2012, science journalist Michael J. Coren describes the effort:

> MIT is trying to crack the wicked problem of teaching literacy and other skills to 100 million or so first-grade-age kids in the developing world with no teachers or infrastructure. Since vast swaths of the world [are] unable to provide even basic education, scalable solutions are needed to complement the long road to achieve universal schooling (something that took the West centuries).[27]

As part of this effort, OLPC gave one thousand Motorola Xoom tablet PCs and solar chargers to first-graders in Ethiopia. OLPC's founder, Nicholas Negroponte, reports:

> We left the boxes in the village. Closed. Taped shut. No instruction, no human being. I thought, the kids will play with the boxes! Within four minutes, one kid not only opened the box, but found the on/off switch. He'd never seen an on/off switch. He powered it up. Within five days, they were using 47 apps per child per day. Within two weeks, they were singing ABC songs [in English] in the village. And within five months, they had hacked Android. Some idiot in our organization or in the Media Lab had disabled the camera! And they figured out it had a camera, and they hacked Android.[28]

About thirteen years earlier Sugata Mitra, the academic who inspired Vikas Swarup's novel (and the eventual Oscar-winning film) *Slumdog Millionaire*, had demonstrated that simply giving kids access to a computer in the slums of Delhi could empower them to learn math and English.

Mitra broke through a wall in the side of a building to provide the local kids in the slum access to a computer, and he left it unsupervised. He was delighted to see that after only a month his Hole in the Wall experiment proved a success: "The kids had taught themselves how to use the computer—boosting their English and math skills at the same time."[29]

Even though it's unclear whether these efforts can be sustained or expanded long term, the immediate results highlight the incredible potential of the younger, prefigurative generations who are already beginning to shape what's coming next. The Ethiopian first-graders who received those Motorola laptops in 2012 are now eighteen or nineteen years old. They represent the heart of Generation Z—a prefigurative generation compelled to adapt to a world shaped by technological advancements unimaginable to their parents and grandparents. The tectonic shift between the post-, co-, and prefigurative generations is shaking the foundations not only of how technology is learned and integrated but also of how younger generations see and process the world.

The expectation for Boomers and Gen Xers was to work hard, put in your time, and eventually reap nice rewards in the form of salary, position, and lifestyle. We were taught—whether we bought into it or not—that the American dream was alive and well and that if we were patient, we'd attain it (via homeownership, an annual vacation, and so on).

What's happening now is that you have the first generations—Gen Z, Alpha, and some younger Millennials—who aren't buying into the old paradigm of the American dream. And it's not necessarily because they don't want to attain the same things the older generations have pursued. It's that many of them believe it is *no longer possible or realistic.*

When it comes to homeownership, for example, there's hard data to show they are right. In 1984 the average American earned $22.4K per year, while the average home in the US cost about $78K. That's a home price-to-income ratio of 3.49. Fast-forward to 2022, when the average American earned $74.6K per year but the average home cost a whopping $433K. That's a ratio of 5.81.[30] Put another way, while salaries have increased about 230 percent, home prices have skyrocketed more than 450 percent. The centerpiece of the American dream—homeownership—has become increasingly difficult to attain for the younger generations.

The key word for this new prefigurative paradigm is *adaptation*. As we mentioned earlier, Margaret Mead made an accurate prediction more than fifty years ago when she said, "In this new culture it will be the child—and not the parent and grandparent—that represents what is to come."[31]

That is happening now. How should the Church respond? The first step is to simply acknowledge that the Church continues to operate with an Industrial-Information frame of reference using postfigurative thinking, while those under forty—particularly Generations Z and Alpha—live and think in an Adaptive/prefigurative world. We must consider form *and* function. The Gospel does not change in form, but the way it functions must adapt. (We will explore this more deeply in the coming chapters.)

**We must consider form *and* function.**

## KEY CHARACTERISTICS OF GENERATION Z

Let's start with the good news: Generation Z is arguably the most entrepreneurial generation in history. They have been born into a time when technology has leveled the playing field, and doors of opportunity are opening where none existed before. Digital developments and tools such as blockchain technology and open-source internet (Web3) have been a seedbed for innovation and advancement for those with the skills and motivation.

Generation Z has also had to adapt to major disruptions over which they had no control. Most were born after 9/11 and into the age of terrorism and its long shadow. School shootings, civil unrest, the COVID-19 pandemic, racial violence, and the nationwide protests after George Floyd's death have heightened this generation's cynicism and made them one of the most hesitant generations in history.

Before they commit, they want to know what their peers think—even more, at times, than what their elders think. Why? Because they have grown up in a postmodern and posttruth era where civility is increasingly uncommon, the world is just as polluted as ever, and climate change is something they've inherited from their grandparents and parents. Politics seems to have devolved into total partisanship, and the cost of living just keeps rising. As they process these bleak realities through a worldview that is prefigurative and adaptive, they turn to one another and their various tribes to make sense of the world.

But is all the news bad for Generation Z? No. As we touched on previously, they are a spiritually open generation that seems hungry for the things of God, and that hunger is on the rise. Here's what Barna Group CEO David Kinnaman has to say of today's younger generations:

> Some of the greatest signs of hope for the Church come from our recent study—our largest one to date—of teens around the world, including in the U.S. Findings from The Open Generation [survey and study] indicate that young people may be fueling this rise in spiritual hunger. Overwhelmingly, Christian teens today say that Jesus still matters to them; 76 percent say "Jesus speaks to me in a way that is relevant to my life."[32]

Many sociologists and NextGen experts predicted that the younger generations would move from the publisher mentality of the Information Age to a creator mentality in this new Adaptive Age. However, that does not seem to be the predominant case. Instead, rather than focusing on publishing, they are concerned with the pathways and means to *adapt* and survive in these complex, intense times.

So yes, while Generation Z (and Alpha) are content creators and publishers who gather in tribes to process what they are publishing, there is a pressing need to understand and employ the rapidly developing tools needed to process what is being published—through posts, clicks, likes, and comments—in order to survive and adapt.

## IMMENSE OPPORTUNITIES FOR THE CHURCH

God's Church has an unprecedented opportunity as we stand on the threshold of the Adaptive Age and slowly transition from the patterns, trends, and advancements of the Information Age. The beautiful central truth of the Gospel is unchanging and unalterable, and we are anchored to its immutable truth even as storms of change rage around us.

■ ■

**This Open Generation is hungry for Jesus.**

■ ■

But to assume that today's youth will respond to Information Age ways of "doing church" is to miss an enormous opportunity. This Open Generation is hungry for Jesus. Are we willing to kill the sacred cows of past ways of doing church in order to capture an entirely new breed of Christian? I know that the answer is yes because I ask it wherever I go, and the answer is always the same.

CHAPTER 5

# Disruption Demands Pioneers

*dis·rup·tion (dis-'rəp-shən): the action of preventing something, especially a system, process, or event, from continuing as usual or as expected*[33]

God's Kingdom does not advance without disruption, and no great move of God has taken place without massive disruption to the status quo. This is the way He works—smashing through our complacency and rebellion to shake and redeem us.

To lay the groundwork for a better understanding of disruption today in all its forms (spiritual, technological, and otherwise) and how the Church can adapt, let's clarify the difference between an interruption and a disruption. From a spiritual perspective,

- an interruption is temporary, while a disruption is lasting;
- an interruption is mildly inconvenient, while a disruption is deeply unsettling;
- an interruption is a distraction, yet a disruption can turn into a visitation;
- an interruption is an eye raiser, and a disruption is a game changer.

**No great move of God has taken place without massive disruption to the status quo.**

## BIBLICAL DISRUPTIONS

Moses' privileged life in Egypt was *interrupted* when the Egyptian soldier beat a Hebrew slave and Moses retaliated. (See Exodus 2:11–12.) But God *disrupted* Moses' new life in Midian when He revealed Himself in the burning bush and commanded Moses to return to Egypt to free His people. This account in Exodus 3 reveals much about Moses (and you and me) as well as the nature of God:

- Moses hides his face when God speaks to him; God makes it clear that He is the one true God of Moses' forefathers.
- Moses is a wanted criminal hiding in the desert; God consecrates the ground as holy and raises him up as a leader.
- Moses is unsure; God reassures Moses that He will go before him.

- Moses lacks confidence; God gives him Aaron to assist him, and later in battle, Aaron and Hur to hold up his arms.

God always makes it difficult for us to feel comfortable when we languish in spiritual deserts. While Satan throws constant interruptions at us—preoccupying us with things other than God, locking us in patterns of shame, or fixating our attention on the wrong things—God relentlessly *disrupts* our lives when they veer off track. He does this for us individually and for the Church as a whole. And I believe that is what He is doing right now in this chaotic and confusing day and age with His Church. It is what He has always done to move His people from the wilderness to His destination for them. His Word is full of examples:

- *The Garden*—When God made Adam and Eve, He disrupted the pre-Adamic order and entered into intimate relationship with His highest creation, whom He gave dominion over the earth. (See Genesis 2:4–3:24.)
- *The Flood*—When God saw that humanity was corrupt, He disrupted the antediluvian order by wiping the slate clean and starting over. (See Genesis 6:9–9:17.)
- *The Tower of Babel*—When God saw the peoples of the earth gathered to defy Him, He disrupted the world by bringing a variety of new languages and scattering the people across the earth. (See Genesis 11:1–9.)
- *The Call of Abraham*—When God spoke to Abraham and called him to be a blessing to all peoples and to prepare the way for the Messiah, He disrupted all that came before and advanced the trajectory of His plan for humankind.
- *Crossing the Jordan*—When God parted the waters of the Jordan, He disrupted the final threads of captivity and then established His people in the Promised Land.

- *The Call of David*—When God plucked the youngest, forgotten son from obscurity, He disrupted a nation.
- *The Birth of Jesus*—When God raised up a poor, unwed teen to give birth to the Messiah, He disrupted the natural order.
- *The Garden of Gethsemane*—When Jesus fully surrendered His destiny, He disrupted the devil's plans to dissuade Him.
- *The Crucifixion*—When Jesus took on the sins of the world, He disrupted the penalty of sin that humanity deserved and took the punishment upon Himself.
- *The Resurrection*—When God raised Jesus from the dead, He disrupted the power of sin and death and secured eternal life for all who believe. This was the greatest disruption in the history of the world.
- *Pentecost*—When the Holy Spirit fell on the 120 believers, He disrupted the earth and gave the Church His indwelling Presence. Before Pentecost, the devil had one Jesus to worry about. On the day of Pentecost he had three thousand "little Jesuses" to worry about.

## JESUS: THE GREAT DISRUPTOR

Jesus is our model of disruption. His entire ministry was one disruption after another: turning water to wine, healing on the Sabbath, breaking bread with sinners, eating with tax collectors, and so on. His Kingdom is one of advancement, of breaking through and moving forward.

**Jesus is our model of disruption.**

When Jesus spoke to John the Baptist's followers, they asked Him if He was the One they had been expecting (the Messiah), and Jesus answered in the affirmative. After they left, He turned to the crowd and said, "From the days of John the Baptist until now, the kingdom of heaven has been subjected to violence, and violent people have been raiding it" (Matthew 11:11–12).

What kind of "violence" is Jesus talking about? We know He did not come to bring a physically violent revolution but a spiritual one. Spiritual passivity does not advance the Kingdom. The Church is called to partner with Christ as He advances His Kingdom. We need to aggressively pursue God's disruption agenda—not by breaking laws but by breaking chains the enemy has placed on people. And we must proclaim the radical message of the Gospel using methods relevant to this generation.

Jesus' version of violence here equates to forcefully advancing—the Kingdom of God must be sought with strong resolve, which is exactly how the Lord operates. There's very little neutrality or status quo in God's plan for us or His Church.

God's Church has always had a mandate to move forward rather than stand still (holding on to models that worked even last year) or look backward to Industrial Age models of attraction (more on this shortly). We must identify what moves and attracts today's youth and young adults and seize upon those containers for our Gospel delivery systems.

## PIONEERS, NOT SETTLERS

Jesus never settled. He pressed, He pushed, He pursued, and He always pioneered. When His disciples were hungry, they gleaned heads of wheat on the Sabbath. When He encountered a crippled man on a pallet, He healed him (again, on the Sabbath). When He was utterly exhausted and hot after a long morning's walk, He stopped at Jacob's well and asked an "untouchable" for a drink of water. It was bad enough that she was an unclean Samaritan, but she was doubly cursed in that she was a five-time divorcée living in sin with her latest partner.

Jesus' approach was so foreign to the established religious order of His day that despite witnessing firsthand many of His miracles and hearing His transformational teaching, they refused to abandon their precious paradigms. As I have said, I love the Church, I am optimistic about its future, and I have dedicated my life to it within a Kingdom context. The main thing we can take away from the Pharisees and Sadducees, however, is that God's Living Water needs and deserves fresh, new containers.

What containers are you using to offer His Living Water to the young people in your sphere of influence? As He said,

> And no one pours new wine into old wineskins. Otherwise, the new wine will burst the skins; the wine will run out and the wineskins will be ruined. No, new wine must be poured into new wineskins.
>
> —Luke 5:37–38

Jesus was no respecter of persons or paradigms. He's our perfect model of how to "do" disruptive, God-honoring ministry to Generations Z, Alpha, and Beta—not using old wineskins that are now outdated and culturally out of touch but new wineskins that understand young people's native mindset and communication language.

## HISTORICAL CHURCH DISRUPTIONS

Since the biblical canon closed at the end of the apostolic period in the first century, there have been thousands of disruptions that allowed God to move His Church forward. Volumes have been filled with these accounts, but for our purposes, a brief overview will help put things into context:

- *Edict of Milan* (313)—Roman Emperor Constantine converted to Christianity and granted religious freedom to Christians and other faiths.
- *Council of Nicaea* (325)—Disputes over Jesus' divinity were addressed; the Nicene Creed was written to affirm the doctrinal truth of the Trinity.
- *The Great Schism* (1054)—The Church split over theological, cultural, and political issues, as the Eastern Church (based in Constantinople) rejected the Roman Pope's claim to supreme authority over all Christians.
- *The Protestant Reformation* (1517)—Martin Luther's 95 Theses challenged such practices as indulgences and the Pope's authority over believers, and new denominations—Lutheran, Reformed, Anglican—sprouted over the next several centuries.
- *The Enlightenment* (seventeenth and eighteenth centuries)—The rise of rationalism, secularism, scientific advancements, and questions of religious authority led to a weakening of institutional Christianity's grip on society.
- *The First and Second Great Awakenings* (1730s–1750s, 1790s–1840s)—These American awakenings, led first by Edwards and Whitefield and later by Finney and Asbury, resulted in great numbers of conversions and significant social reform.
- *The Welsh Revival and the Azusa Street Revival* (1904–1905, 1906)—Though thousands of miles apart, the Welsh Revival inspired many across the Atlantic to pray for a similar move of God. In Los Angeles the Azusa Street Revival was accompanied by signs and wonders and marked the birth of modern Pentecostalism.

- *The Billy Graham Crusades and the Rise of Evangelicalism* (1950s–1990s)—With the rise of evangelicalism in America, disruptions occurred through the emergence of attractional evangelism and discipleship models and the increasing influence of religion in politics.
- *The Jesus Movement* (late 1960s–early 1970s)—A revival led by Smith, Frisbee, and others broke out among hippies and counterculture youth in America, emphasizing a personal relationship with Jesus. It led to the rise of contemporary Christian music (CCM) and the growth of megachurches.
- *The Third Wave and Global Charismatic Revival* (1980s–present)—Since the 1980s there has been massive growth in Pentecostalism and Charismatic Christianity worldwide. Latin America, Africa, and Asia have become the heartlands of Christian revival, with explosive growth in places such as the Underground House Church Movement in China. Prominent global leaders include Reinhard Bonnke (Africa), Peter Wagner and John Wimber (United States), Hillsong (Australia), and Bethel Church (Redding, California).

**There have been thousands of disruptions that allowed God to move His Church forward.**

Though by no means an exhaustive list, this provides a bird's-eye view of some of the major disruptions that have influenced the Church over the past two thousand years. To fully grasp what is happening today in the Church, particularly as it relates to younger generations,

I believe it's critical to keep both biblical history and the Church's history at the forefront of our minds.

## THE ATTRACTIONAL MYTH

Honing in on the past seventy-five years, in particular, we saw the birth of evangelicalism in the US and the growth of the megachurch and parachurch movements. After the Great Depression and World War II, Americans were ready for consistency and normality, and local churches sprang up in newly minted suburbs of large cities across the US. The approach to church attendance was attractional, meaning if the right factors were pursued and achieved, the pews would fill.

Keep in mind that in every three or four generations, an attractional model emerges because the Church finds something they love and then puts it on repeat. Following World War II, the Church was in dreadful need of an update.

The key factors of attractional ministry and church growth theory are

1] excellent Bible teaching,
2] attractive facilities,
3] programs to accommodate all phases of life, including excellent children's Sunday school classes (e.g., children's church), and
4] professional-level worship.

The attractional model is very much based on an Industrial-Information Age mindset and postfigurative/cofigurative thinking—value is based on what we do as churches, and learning trickles down from elders to younger generations. This was particularly seen in the rise of megachurches starting in the late 1960s and 1970s, with gorgeous, large auditoriums, excellent worship music, and top-notch preachers recruited from the nation's prestigious seminaries. Size mattered. Facilities mattered. Numbers mattered. Was (or is) this a flawed model? Overall, I don't believe so. It was a model that worked well for decades.

That is, until it didn't.

Between 2000 and 2015 mainline denominations such as the Presbyterian Church (U.S.A.), the Episcopal Church, and the United Church of Christ lost 40 percent of their members. Interestingly, evangelical churches saw a slight gain in memberships. Overall, however, church membership has steadily declined since the turn of the century.[34]

The era-defining disruptions of the COVID-19 pandemic period only accelerated the downward trend, as many of us attended church online (or at least acted like we did), and many former regular church members did not attend at all. I say "pandemic period" because 2020–2022 also saw the explosion of civil unrest following the death of George Floyd, the January 6 attack on the US Capitol, widening political animus, the outbreak of the Russo-Ukrainian war, and the crescendo of the #MeToo movement. Though it has been an especially fractious and intense five-plus-year period for everyone, it served to drive the younger generations more deeply into their familiar, native landscape and language: digital Babylon, where everyone speaks the same online language or dialects thereof. (This is a key topic in the next chapter.)

Particularly after the seismic cultural events that have shaken us in the '20s, Generation Z is not as interested in church programs (preaching, teaching, facilities, etc.) as they are in this question: *How can your church show me how to survive and adapt in a culture that is increasingly apathetic toward the Gospel, is embracing posttruth and pre-Christian norms, and is divided along political and cultural lines?*

For Generations Z, Alpha, and soon Beta, the attractional model has sailed.

It's not that it was a bad or flawed model; it simply is not a model that works well with the younger generations. It worked for Baby Boomers and Generation X (and older Millennials) because it catered to the way we acquired knowledge and learning (postfigurative/cofigurative) and what we valued in a world that was transitioning from the Industrial Age ("What do you do?") to the Information Age ("What do you think?").

**For Generations Z, Alpha, and soon Beta, the attractional model has sailed.**

Emerging from the horrors of World War II, the rise of Communism, and the Cold War, the nation was ready for consistency and safety. That is what they got in their churches, for the most part. But with the Cuban Missile Crisis, the Vietnam War, and violence surrounding the Civil Rights Movement, things turned dark again. That's when God used disruption to soften the hearts of a nation searching for "peace" in all the wrong places (e.g., the hippie movement and sexual revolution) and the Jesus Movement exploded across the US.

As I write this, the Russo-Ukrainian war rages on as the Ukrainians continue to punch well above their weight, fighting the world's second-largest military in a bloody stalemate. Americans across the political spectrum are tearing each other to shreds, and propaganda seems to be at an all-time high from both domestic sources and overseas infiltrators. And in the Church, the fissures along political and philosophical lines grow deeper and wider.

All the while, our young people look on, disoriented by the animosity plaguing every corner of our country, including inside our churches.

It's a perfect opportunity for leaders to step up—to learn to speak the younger generations' language and walk into the breach. I believe it's a *kairos* moment unlike any we have seen in the US in fifty years.

As we discussed in the previous chapter, today's digital landscape is made up of disparate but connected people gathering virtually around various hives of information and then taking the pollen to other hives and tribes. These hives of mutual experience may or may not be based in reality, but in our posttruth society, emotions and thoughts often overshadow facts and truth.

"What is truth?" is the mantra that echoes into the digital terrain. Who is answering back? Mostly, their peers and secularists who say, "There is none. Go make your own." We must counter this false gospel and bring the love and relevance of the Gospel we know to be the truth. That is our calling at this specific time in history.

It's the Church's job to provide the answer to that age-old question, speaking to the virtual residents of digital Babylon in the language they understand. To wait for them to learn our language—postfigurative, attractional, and Information Age–oriented—is unrealistic. They aren't, and they won't. Attractional models won't work on adaptive thinkers.

**Attractional models won't work on adaptive thinkers.**

We must go to them. We must converse with them in phrases and words they understand. We must adapt on behalf of the adapters. Their language is entirely native to Generation Z and totally foreign to most Millennials, Gen Xers, and Boomers. It's the exact time for "those of a certain age" to take a good, hard look at what tools we've been using to try to get the younger generations to come and stay in our churches.

What do the younger generations want?

- Leaders who can help them make sense of the posttruth culture and become culturally discerning using the truth of the Gospel.
- Experienced teachers to help them move past the consumer phase of Christianity into the disciple phase—a real experience that does not sugarcoat the commitment it takes to be a genuine, surrendered disciple of Jesus.
- Guides to disciple them, help them move as Jesus would in today's climate, and reach their native generation in their own language while using the Word as the filter.
- Mentors to help them understand and navigate the cynical, post-truth world they live in, providing support, encouragement, and biblical training to adapt and thrive in the Adaptive Age.

The fact is that every generation is different from the next, and the need for adaptation has always been a constant. The difference now, however, is that full revolutions of change (e.g., from the '50s-era youth culture to the hippie culture of the mid- and late '60s) that used to take fifteen or twenty years to complete are now happening *within* a generation. In other words, as digital speeds and improvements accelerate at unprecedented rates, technology advances rapidly, leading to the very fast turnover of cultural trends.

Think this sounds overwhelming? You are not alone. However, as we get to know what makes people under thirty tick—how they think, what they value, and what they believe—we gain the critical knowledge we need to make the necessary adaptations. But knowledge can't remain in a vacuum. When paired with the power of the Holy Spirit and the wisdom that flows only from Him, the Church can—and will—make the critically needed adjustments.

Half a century after the Jesus Movement, the nation is ripe for another major move of holy disruption. In this moment what is your role? What is mine? We will explore those questions in the coming chapters.

CHAPTER 6

# Exiled for a Purpose

*The truth is like a lion; you don't have to defend it. Let it loose; it will defend itself.*
—AUTHOR UNKNOWN

When we approach the younger generations with the Gospel, we do not need to apologize for its truth. Though that quote has been commonly misattributed to St. Augustine (while the original source remains unknown), its power still resonates. We need not soft-pedal the truth.

Jesus is constant; His truth is unchanging. To represent Him as anything else is not only unbiblical but also illogical to a generation drowning in relativism while hungry and thirsty for truth. Just as you don't throw a drowning man half a life preserver, you do not withhold the fullness of the Gospel.

**Just as you don't throw a drowning man half a life preserver, you do not withhold the fullness of the Gospel.**

The need for adaptation is not about the Gospel's power or lack thereof (its power is eternal and consistent) but about its *presentation*, which is temporal and changing. The Gospel will always take the shape of the container it fills. When you pour pure water into a mug or bottle, its purity remains even as its shape conforms to the shape of the container. The Gospel does the same: It takes the shape of whatever context it's in without diluting itself or compromising its message, accomplishing the mission of redemption. In other words, we study and discern the language of the younger generations in the context of today's Babylon and translate the Gospel in a way that meets them *in that place*. God has tasked us as the Church with providing an accurate and clear presentation of the Gospel in a sociocultural language that Generations Z and Alpha can understand.

Changing methods does not mean surrendering the clarity or power of the Gospel. That's a false binary. There's no need to give these generations anything but the pure, unfiltered water of the Gospel.

## A LIGHT IN BABYLON

As in ancient Babylon, there are stark contrasts between the paganism surrounding today's younger generations and the level of faith necessary to hold to one's religious convictions. We will dive more into this subject in the next chapter when we examine how a particular remnant of the exiled Jews not only survived in Babylon but also thrived—culturally and spiritually.

And similar to Babylon, I believe God is especially preparing Generations Z and Alpha (and soon Beta) not only to navigate today's Babylon-like culture but also to win their peers to Christ in large numbers. He is stirring a hunger in their hearts for the authentic Jesus—beyond the religious institutions and structures that have served the Church for the past half century. As those outdated methods fade away, new methods—new wineskins—will emerge. It is in this context that the older generations can and must partner with the younger generations to see His purposes and plans fulfilled.

Jesus is raising up a new generation of worshippers who are seeking Him, and it is our responsibility to embrace them, serve them, and help them become salt and light in today's digital and cultural Babylon.

## LEARNING FROM THE PAST

In 1905 Spanish-American philosopher George Santayana wrote, "Those who cannot remember the past are condemned to repeat it."[35] Such sentiment is highly relevant for the Church today.

Immediately after September 11, 2001, the United States was in crisis, and there was a brief surge in church attendance and spiritual engagement. But over the next two decades the statistics were not kind to Christianity in the US. As we already discussed, Christian identity declined at alarming rates during those twenty years. The 2023–24 Religious Landscape Study finally offered a glimmer of hope, showing a significant slowing of the decline. And the glimmer quickly grew into a glow with Barna Group's most recent survey results, published in April 2025:

> According to Barna's latest data, 66 percent of all U.S. adults say they have made a personal commitment to Jesus that is still important in their life today. That marks a 12-percentage-point increase since 2021, when commitment levels reached their lowest in more than three decades of Barna tracking.[36]

That is incredible news, and as the Barna Group puts it:

> This shift is not only statistically significant—it may be the clearest indication of meaningful spiritual renewal in the United States. Commitment to Jesus was lowest in 2021 and 2022, when it bottomed out at 54 percent. Since then, the research shows a steady, year-over-year increase in the key indicator.[37]

While we can rejoice over this news, it's also important that we remain realistic. Spiritual renewal brings with it a significant responsibility for the Church and its leaders to implement methodologies that welcome new believers into the pews and adaptive practices that keep them there.

■ ■

**Spiritual renewal brings with it a significant responsibility for the Church and its leaders.**

■ ■

As I mentioned previously, I'm not pessimistic about the state of the Church or its future. I am hopefully realistic. Major disruptions are upon us, and as such, major adaptations are required—not so the Church can survive (it will), but so it can thrive in its *mission* (which is up to us), as evidenced by Gen Z.

In order to better process the present with realistic lenses and strategically project what is coming, I want to examine a culture that had striking similarities to ours. It too contained a remnant of faith-filled people who lived, worshipped, and worked in a highly advanced, spiritually diverse, predominantly pagan society. With a nod to Santayana, we will examine history in order to inform the present so we can best evangelize and disciple the most spiritually open generation in decades.

To provide insights into today's "American Babylon," let's take a moment to explore the *original* Babylon—a city (first) and civilization (later). Though the Babylonian empire existed more than twenty-five hundred years ago, it has much to tell us about today's complex and chaotic digital age.

## BABEL AND REBELLION

The first mention of Babel (as a place, before it became a city or an empire) is in Genesis 10. After the Flood, Noah's descendants settled on the plain of Shinar, a region between the Tigris and Euphrates Rivers. Often called the Cradle of Civilization, this area is where God wanted mankind to rebuild and worship Him in obedience. Noah's great-grandson Nimrod "became a mighty warrior on the earth. . . . The first centers of his kingdom were Babylon, Uruk, Akkad and Kalneh, in Shinar" (Genesis 10:8, 10).

Nimrod was one of the region's earliest kings, according to Jewish historian Josephus. In his classic work *The Antiquities of the Jews*, completed in AD 94 (shortly before John the apostle's death), Josephus describes Nimrod's rebellion against God:

> He [Nimrod] also said he would be revenged on God, if he should have a mind to drown the world again; for that he would build a

> tower for the waters to be able to reach! and that he would avenge himself on God for destroying their forefathers![38]

The Second Temple writings (between the sixth century BC and the destruction of the Temple in AD 70) and the Talmud (AD 300–600) both identify Nimrod as the leader who commissioned the construction of the Tower of Babel. Genesis says,

> Now the whole world had one language and a common speech. As people moved eastward, they found a plain in Shinar and settled there. They said to each other, "Come, let's make bricks and bake them thoroughly." They used brick instead of stone, and tar for mortar. Then they said, "Come, let us build ourselves a city, with a tower that reaches to the heavens, so that we may make a name for ourselves; otherwise we will be scattered over the face of the whole earth."
>
> —Genesis 11:1–4

Instead of building in reverence to God, the residents of Babel built their tower to challenge His authority and assert their own power. As a result of their rebellion, God moved against them:

> But the LORD came down to see the city and the tower the people were building. The LORD said, "If as one people speaking the same language they have begun to do this, then nothing they plan to do will be impossible for them. Come, let us go down and confuse their language so they will not understand each other." So the LORD scattered them from there over all the earth, and they stopped building the city. That is why it was called Babel—because there the LORD confused the language of the whole world. From there the LORD scattered them over the face of the whole earth.
>
> —Genesis 11:5–9

What was God's motivation? Fear? Hate? Neither. After the Flood, God desired a fresh start for His creation. I believe He cared so much for the people that He did what was best for them: He disrupted their current state of living—stained with pride and arrogance—and dispersed them across the earth, giving them separate languages.

Major disruption was needed to realign people's hearts with His purposes. He's doing the same thing today: disrupting the old attractional ways of doing ministry and opening the eyes of today's leaders to go into the streets and neighborhoods to reach the younger generations exactly where they live, work, and play.

**Major disruption was needed to realign people's hearts with His purposes.**

Just as the Word says that God cares about the nations (see Matthew 28:19–20), so too *He loves cities*. Why? Because they are full of His most beloved creation: people! He cared for the pagan city of Nineveh so much that He sent Jonah to preach the Word there. Jesus loved Jerusalem and His fellow Jews, and He wept over the city because many had rejected the truth (see Luke 19:41–44).

Similarly, God cared about the people of Babel—so much so, in fact, that He dismantled their monolinguistic power structure, scattered them into tribes and groups, and gave them different languages. His mission was found in His original command to "be fruitful and multiply and fill the earth" (Genesis 1:28, ESV). And that's the core of disruption: God uses it to realign His people with His intended mission.

When God brings disruption, it's rarely for disruption's sake; rather, it's for the sake of mission. His desire was that many nations would collectively be in relationship with Him.

Unfortunately, that is not what happened.

As the people's rebellion continued, another disruption was in order, and we read about it in Genesis 12:1–3:

> The LORD had said to Abram, "Go from your country, your people and your father's household to the land I will show you. I will make you into a great nation, and I will bless you; I will make your name great, and you will be a blessing. I will bless those who bless you, and whoever curses you I will curse; and all peoples on earth will be blessed through you."

Note that Abraham was from the region of Ur (in present-day southern Iraq), which at the time—approximately 2000 BC—was its own dynasty, as Babylon was not yet an empire or a dominant power in Mesopotamia. As we've said, in each generation God raises up a remnant of faithful followers whom He uses in His disruption plan. For that time, God chose a couple from Ur of the Chaldeans, not far from where Nimrod had built his tower.

According to Jewish tradition, Abraham came from a family of idol makers (*Genesis Rabbah 38:*13) who practiced idol worship.[39] But God saw something different in Abraham—He saw his heart. And Abraham responded to God's call. We know the rest of the story: God used Abraham to birth the faith of the Jewish people and to plant a spiritual tree into which all Christians have been grafted. By every measure, Abraham was a major adapter in one of God's greatest sagas of disruption.

Here's something else for those of us forty and above to think about: God didn't give Abraham and Sarah a child until they were much older, yet He said their descendants—both genetic and spiritual sons and daughters—would be "as numerous as the stars in the sky and as the sand on the seashore" (Genesis 22:17; see also 15:5).

As we pray about the role we are to play in raising up the younger generations, we must resist the temptation to believe we are "too old" or otherwise unqualified. God will use anyone at any age to fulfill His purposes—all He needs is a willing heart. But before He can use any of us in His disruption plans, we must allow Him to disrupt our own hearts so we can be used as vessels for adaptation.

■ ■

**We must allow Him to disrupt our own hearts so we can be used as vessels for adaptation.**

■ ■

Everything we do, then, is based on praying for, discerning, and pursuing God's mission. *Everything.*

God's mission for Abraham was to use him to give birth to a nation. For the next fourteen hundred years, until its subjugation and subsequent exile to Babylon, the people of Israel endured one disruption after another. Some of these disruptions were catastrophic due to their own sins (particularly idolatry), and some were positive, as a remnant thread was present in every generation—just like today and, as we will see, just like in Babylon.

Through God's "stiff-necked people," His mission never changed—the people's hearts did. As with earlier disruptions that shifted history to align with God's mission—the Flood, Babel, the Red Sea crossing—God was once again about to do something radical.

# MISSION OVER IDOLS

After the reigns of Kings David and Solomon (the latter's reign ended in 931 BC), Israel quickly devolved into civil war and eventually split—the kingdom of Israel in the north and the newly formed kingdom of Judah in the south. Over the next three hundred years Judah shrank in both power and influence, and only four of its twenty rulers remained faithful to the Lord.

By the time of King Josiah (640–609 BC), Judah was spiritually and politically fragile. Josiah was the last righteous king before the exile, and although he led sincere religious reforms, the people continued to run after idols and refused to fully turn back to the Lord. After Josiah's death, surrounding powers seized the opportunity presented by weak leadership. Egypt installed Jehoiakim as a puppet king, but soon after, Babylon defeated Egypt at Carchemish in 605 BC and asserted its dominance over Judah.

That same year, the prophet Jeremiah gave his sobering warning:

> "This whole country will become a desolate wasteland, and these nations will serve the king of Babylon seventy years. But when the seventy years are fulfilled, I will punish the king of Babylon and his nation, the land of the Babylonians, for their guilt," declares the Lord, "and will make it desolate forever."
>
> —Jeremiah 25:11–12

Despite this and many other prophetic warnings, the people of Judah still refused to repent. In short, God's mission through His people had faltered through their divisions and sins.

On the surface we could evaluate this period as basic dusty history. But there's something profound going on here. As Babylon's control expanded, they began deporting the Jewish elites. They put rings through their noses and chains through those rings and marched the captives nine hundred miles across the desert to the city of Babylon.

These Jews were the best, the brightest, and the wealthiest (in today's terms, the biggest influencers, captains of industry, celebrities, and politicians), and they were all dragged out of Israel.

Why?

*Because Israel had ceased to be the nation God created it to be.*

Israel was supposed to be a city on a hill. The people of Israel were supposed to be the light of the world. They were supposed to be the priests and spiritual leaders, pointing other cities and nations to the one true God.

Instead, Israel built a wall around itself and shut out the rest of the world. And for us today, whether as a believer, church, or ministry, when you build a wall around yourself, the very next steps are idolatry, ethnocentrism, and self-worship—just like the Tower of Babel.

Ironic, isn't it? That same Babel, which was built in rebellion, eventually grew into the empire of Babylon that would capture the Jews and bring them back to the same idolatrous culture the Lord had sought to redeem. It was as if God was saying to Israel, "Oh, no you don't. You are My people, and I am going to put you back into the world. I am going to put you in the most opulent, idol-filled city so you can show the people the one true God."

The Israelites had chosen idols over mission. They'd sacrificed their destiny by walling themselves off from the very world the Lord wanted them to reach with His message of redemption—because His mission is ultimately about redemption.

That's exactly why God stopped the Tower of Babel. He knew that if all humankind fixed their eyes on what they built, they would take their eyes off Him. Whenever a church, a ministry, or a generation of leaders starts to build a wall around itself, the very next step is to idolize it. And that's what happened in Israel.

They built the Temple, and then they idolized the Temple.

Likewise today, the Church cannot isolate itself from the current culture or the broader world. To ignore the realities around us is to commit the same mistakes made by Judah before and after the reign of King Josiah. Through their isolation they ignored the dangers around them (and very specific prophecies from Jeremiah, which we will see in the next chapter) and became susceptible to invasion.

**The Church cannot isolate itself from the current culture or the broader world.**

We must not forget biblical history, or we will risk missing God's mission for the Church today. (His mission always includes the younger generations!) We must open our eyes, grasp a deeper understanding of the disruptions taking place, and embrace an adaptive mindset focused on the evangelization and discipleship of Generations Z and Alpha.

## EXILED FOR A PURPOSE

Among the first wave of Jewish elites deported to Babylon in 605 BC was a 15-year-old boy from a prominent family, along with his three friends. Their names were Daniel, Hananiah, Mishael, and Azariah.[40] In those days it was not uncommon for the sons of prominent households to be taken captive by a conquering nation. Raised under the religious reforms of the late King Josiah, Daniel and his peers knew one religion and one culture. They were a people set apart, who eschewed foreign beliefs and values and embraced a strict adherence to the Torah.

As we will dive more deeply into in the next chapter, it's remarkable how a deported band of exiled Jews, including teenagers and young adults, managed to navigate massive disruption, adapt to a hostile foreign culture, and effect monumental changes. Their story is not unlike ours today in America, with teenagers and twenty-somethings learning to navigate a churning engine of paganism and idolatry fed by rapid technological change.

The story of ancient Babylon reveals how God's people—a remnant of the exiles—were able to adapt and influence those in positions of great power. More specifically, there was a powerful movement in Babylon led by the young leaders Daniel and Ezekiel and their peers.

God has often used young people in His disruption plans. He did it with David, with Mary, with Esther, and with Jesus. When Jesus was just twelve years old, His parents found Him conversing with the rabbis in the Temple. In the modern era God worked similarly with the Jesus Movement, and today He's lighting spiritual fires across college campuses in the US, where youth revivals have been springing up.

It's amazing and encouraging that even in days like today—times that seem so spiritually dark and divided—the Lord is using the younger generations to amplify His message, just as He did in ancient Babylon.

## CHAPTER 7

# Mission to Babylon: Yesterday and Today

*"Seek the peace and prosperity of the city to which I have carried you into exile. Pray to the* LORD *for it, because if it prospers, you too will prosper."*
—JEREMIAH 29:7

Countless times throughout biblical (and postbiblical) history we see darkness turn into opportunity for God's people. In this chapter I want to explore the culture the Jewish exiles were exposed to when they were taken captive and deported to Babylon. As we will see, God had a specific mission: He took an otherwise dire situation and used it to prepare His people for the coming of Jesus some six hundred years later.

We will look at Babylon through an eternal lens—both for the Jews twenty-five hundred years ago and for us today. I believe it's highly relevant as we consider our role to raise up the younger generations—the people of God who will lead the Church after we are gone—in the midst of this pagan culture.

When we look around at the world and the state of the Church in the US, it can leave us feeling a bit helpless and frustrated. Cognitively, we know how the story ends—with Jesus' triumphant return and the Church's victory. But until then it can be hard to keep sowing seeds into the tough soil of today's culture. That's why the story of the Babylonian Exile is so important and relevant: It gives us a holy prototype of how God works in the most difficult climates and provides timeless principles for us today.

## A NATION NOT UNLIKE OUR OWN

At its height in the late seventh and early sixth centuries BC, Babylon was arguably the greatest city in the world. Rome was thriving but had not yet reached its zenith, while Athens had established itself as a center of philosophy and art. Babylon had wealth beyond measure, military might, religious diversity, cultural sophistication, impressive learning institutions and scholarship, and a population of more than two hundred thousand—making it the largest city in the world at the time of the Exile.

At its height Babylon was a civilization not unlike our own, especially as interpreted from the point of view of the Jewish exiles. They were a remnant of outsiders living in a sophisticated, complex, and pagan environment. The comparisons between our modern culture and ancient Babylon are numerous, especially as they pertain to the complexity and speed at which the Jews in ancient Babylon had to adapt, just as today's youth are having to adapt as well.

In the following overview of the two cultures, the goal is to understand the younger generations right where they live, rather than where we live (in terms of the very different environment we were raised in). Hopefully, this will provide context for us as we engage and partner with Generations Z and Alpha.

## GLOBALISM AND ASSIMILATION

### Babylon's Exiles

One of the reasons Babylon rose to prominence was its strategic location on trade routes connecting the East with the West. Over the centuries, it became a multicultural and multiethnic melting pot, with the Sumerians, Akkadians, and later Amorites, Kassites, and Chaldeans all playing significant roles in its history and culture. Then came the first of several waves of exiled Jews in the late seventh and early sixth centuries BC—at the height of the city's splendor—who brought monotheism and their own specific culture and belief system.

God's message to the Jews was entirely missional: "If you're not willing to be a light to the world from Jerusalem, I will take you out of Jerusalem and plant you in the biggest city in the world. You will reach the world from that place." So they landed in Babylon, the nexus of technology, knowledge, and globalization.

The Jews were disrupted and deported from a regional location where only a few languages were spoken and almost everyone kept strict dietary and sacrificial laws. Now they had to adjust to a new reality in a global city where people spoke more than a dozen languages from all over the known world—as far away as modern-day Turkey and India. Instead of accepting their mission and becoming a light, the Jews separated themselves from the rest of Babylon and moved to the outskirts of the city. They chose to blame Babylon for their problems rather than repenting and becoming who God created them to be as a nation. Instead of fulfilling God's mission to reach the people of Babylon in the heart of the city, they retreated to the ghettos and outer districts.

But watch what God did. Rather than reinforce the Jews' desire to remain separated from pagan society and cast blame on Babylon, He revealed that it wasn't Babylon who exiled them—it was *Him*. His desire wasn't for them to live on the outskirts of the society they needed to reach but to move into that city and redeem it. God said,

> This is what the LORD Almighty, the God of Israel, says to all those I carried into exile from Jerusalem to Babylon: "Build houses and settle down; plant gardens and eat what they produce. Marry and have sons and daughters; find wives for your sons and give your daughters in marriage, so that they too may have sons and daughters. Increase in number there; do not decrease. Also, seek the peace and prosperity of the city to which I have carried you into exile. Pray to the LORD for it, because if it prospers, you too will prosper."
>
> —Jeremiah 29:4–7

This was a master class in cultural assimilation for the sake of mission. The Lord showed the Jews exactly how He wanted them to evangelize the city of Babylon. God explained, "The Babylonians didn't do this—I did this. I want you to move back into that dark city, settle in it, be a light in a dark place, increase, and pray for its peace and prosperity."

What a word for believers today! What would happen if we stopped separating ourselves from those we are supposed to reach? What would happen if instead of decreasing our influence because culture isn't doing what we like, we increased our influence and shined the light of Christ? What would happen if instead of complaining about the world, politicians, sin, the economy, and so on, we *prayed* for the peace and prosperity of the places where God has planted us? Well, God tells us exactly what would happen: *Everything we touch would prosper, as it would cause our contexts to prosper as well.*

■ ■

**What would happen if we stopped separating ourselves from those we are supposed to reach?**

■ ■

What better witness could there be to a lost, dark world than to show that the people of God have a better way? I'm always struck by the fact that rather than trying to attract this city full of pagans by using the Jews' own culture and language, God told them to assimilate. It's a vital lesson for us today: We must go to the world, rather than expect them to come to us. Also, it's amazing how God tied the exiles' prosperity to that of Babylon—the nation whose people put the rings and chains on them!

The Babylonians forced the exiles to break their Mosaic laws and customs by shaving their beards and heads and wearing strange clothes and mixed fabrics. They were forced to learn the ways of Babylon to the extent that they looked more Babylonian than Jewish. And even though these practices were against the Law God gave His people, He didn't stop it.

Here's why: God was more concerned with His mission than the culture and convenience of His people. Wear different clothes, eat different foods, and assimilate—just keep your heart turned toward the Lord at all times. Too often we tie our religion—our faith in

Christ—to politics, a nation, or a culture instead of God Himself. He knew that if the exiles' hearts were not properly aligned, they'd be unwilling to assimilate.

God stripped His people of their cultural trappings because they had begun to worship things other than Him. They believed they were secure because they were the people of God who lived in the land of God (in the city of God) and worshipped in the house of God. Their identity was in their location more than in their Creator. So God plucked them out of their homeland and said, "You are going to be who you are not because of where you live but because of who you are in Me and My mission. THAT'S your identity."

People like Ezekiel (only twenty-five when he was deported to Babylon) and Daniel, Mishael, Hananiah, and Azariah (all teenagers) did not give in to the temptations of Babylon but remained true to the Lord. That's the key: *They assimilated without sacrificing their mission. They adapted.*

Yes, Daniel took his famous fast of vegetables and water, but he also served four different kings: Nebuchadnezzar and Belshazzar before Babylon fell, and Darius and Cyrus after Persia took over.

Daniel and his friends even received new Babylonian names from Nebuchadnezzar's chief official. Daniel became Belteshazzar, which means "Bel protect the king" (Bel being a Babylonian god).[41] Hananiah, Mishael, and Azariah became the names we know them by today: Shadrach, Meshach, and Abednego (see Daniel 1:6–7).

When God gives us a calling, it doesn't matter what others call us.

■ ■

**When God gives us a calling, it doesn't matter what others call us.**

■ ■

What matters is what God has called us to be and do. What names do we attribute to the younger generations?

"Lazy."

"Unreliable."

"Ungodly."

We need to be careful to call them what God wants them to be, rather than label them through filters of our own making. In Daniel's case he stayed true to his original calling and lived up to the meaning of his Hebrew name: "God is my judge."

**Today's Generation**

In June 2025 the US Census Bureau released the following information based on data collected between 2017 and 2021:

- There were "over 500 individual languages and languages groups spoken across the country during this time."
- "More than 1 in 5 people (22%) age 5 and older in the United States spoke a language other than English at home."
- "Among people who spoke a language other than English, approximately 61% spoke Spanish and 78% spoke an Indo-European language (including, among others, Spanish, German, French and Italian)."
- "Sixty-two percent of those who spoke a language other than English at home also spoke English 'very well.'"[42]

Also, according to Pew Research Center, "Immigrants today account for 14.3% of the U.S. population, a roughly threefold increase from 4.7% in 1970. The immigrant share of the population today is the highest since 1910 but remains below the record 14.8% in 1890."[43] In other words, not since the height of the great migrations from Europe during the Industrial Age have so many diverse cultures descended upon our shores. This is very similar to what was happening in ancient Babylon at the time of the Exile.

**Similarities**

*Culture shock* would be a gross understatement for what the exiles experienced upon their arrival in Babylon. The culture in Judah was one set apart—a people and religion isolated from other cultures on purpose. But what they found in the world's most sophisticated city was a melting pot of people groups, cultures, and religions. The Jews' task was to remain faithful to the one true God while assimilating and succeeding as strangers in a strange land. This is Missiology 101: bearing the *imago Dei* and being a witness to the ends of the earth. Today, young Americans are adapting to changes their parents couldn't have imagined as they encounter cultural pluralism unlike any in the history of the US. Honestly, it's hard for us older believers to fully wrap our heads around how different culture is now compared with how it was when we were growing up in the '60s–'80s.

## TECHNOLOGICAL ADVANCEMENT AND COMPETITION

**Babylon's Exiles**

The list of inventions and technological breakthroughs credited to the Babylonian Empire is long and impressive. Starting with the early Babylonians and their precursors (3000 BC and earlier), they pioneered discoveries such as the wheel, the chariot, and the sailboat, as well as the development of the first-known map. Other improvements include advanced geometry and astronomy, innovations in irrigation, and the construction of double-leveled walls (parallel walls separated by a moat to protect against invaders) all around Babylon.

Babylonian advancements went beyond math, science, and warfare and included the Code of Hammurabi (one of the earliest legal codes, written c. 1750 BC), the legendary Hanging Gardens (described as having watercourses and fountains), and the massive Etemenanki ziggurat (a pyramid-like structure with squared-off edges, constructed of mud brick and baked brick).[44] Cuneiform (the first written language) was developed by the Sumerians in the late fourth millennium BC, but the Babylonians adapted and improved it significantly.[45] Similarly, the Babylonians inherited the Sumerians' sexagesimal system (measuring time and angles in units of 60) and expanded its use to include astronomy, complex mathematical calculations, and calendar systems.[46]

These wonders must have caused the exiles' heads to spin. They were forced to adapt not only to a new language and culture but also to technology they'd never dreamed of before. (Sound familiar?)

### Today's Generation

The same can be said of the average American today. There's no question that the past one hundred years—and particularly the past fifty years—in the US have seen more technological advancements than any other century in world history. We've already touched on many of the technological highlights of the twentieth and early twenty-first centuries, so suffice it to say that the rate at which new breakthroughs are coming—especially in digital technology—is accelerating. More discoveries are being made each year.

This is both wonderful and concerning. It's wonderful because both the quality and average length of life are on the rise. There are major advances in cancer research, brain science, and disease prevention. But it's concerning too when you consider the real issues of screen addiction, social isolation, and rising rates of mental illness. The speed of technological advancements, coupled with the stress of living in today's divisive and competitive culture, makes adaptation that much more critical.

The younger generations have more "adult stuff" thrown at them earlier and faster than people over forty did at the same age. On top of that, it's a very competitive world from the education process to the job market. For example, I have a friend who went to an all-boys Catholic prep high school and was admitted to UCLA with a 3.4 GPA and a 1040 SAT. He attended UCLA from 1981–1985 and earned a bachelor's degree in English literature. My friend reported that the "all-in" cost was approximately $10,000 per year.

Today, UCLA receives more college applications than any other university in the world. For the fall 2024 cycle there were 146,271 first-year applicants, and the acceptance rate was 9 percent.[47] The average high school GPA for admitted students was 4.18-4.3, and though no longer considered in the admissions process, the average SAT score ranged from 1290 to 1510.[48] And the cost? Even though UCLA is a public university, the price tag for California residents is around $40,000—a 400 percent increase since 1981.[49] Across town at the University of Southern California (USC), which is a private university, the price tag is a whopping $95,000 per year![50]

The shift in a person's college experience in only forty years is just one example of how much things have changed. It's fairly radical, and it shows how different the college costs and admission processes are for Baby Boomers versus Generation Z. For new generations—especially with the cost of education and the fact that one's degree becomes redundant even before graduation (due to the speed of technology)—the goal is not so much to attain an education but to hack one. (We will discuss this more in the next chapter.)

### Similarities (Don't miss this!)

Three crucial things came together in Babylon that are reflected in today's culture:

1] Technology
2] Knowledge
3] Globalization

No city up to that time had so profoundly advanced along these three rails of civilization. It's much like today, where these same factors have produced the most savvy, cautious, and hesitant generations in decades—all from the convenience of "smart devices." The nexus of these three factors may have occurred off and on throughout history, but now, with the advent of the internet, there is no "off switch"—short of a complete global shutdown of electricity and the internet (which isn't very likely).

As technological innovations multiply, knowledge sharing and building compounds exponentially, and as a result, the globalized utilization of both these factors contributes to a more connected and shared world. Again, there's no off switch for this. It makes me think of Margaret Mead's words regarding cultural transmission:

> I call this new style prefigurative because in this new culture it will be the child—and not the parent and grandparent—that represents what is to come.[51]
>
> We are now fully living in that time.
>
> What is our response?

In a similar climate, the Jewish exiles found themselves with a mandate from God to "seek the peace and prosperity of the city to which I have carried you into exile. Pray to the Lord for it, because if it prospers, you too will prosper" (Jeremiah 29:7). This is the exact same mandate God gives us today: to go into the city, rather than retreat into our churches; to immerse ourselves in the digital spaces occupied by today's youth, rather than distance ourselves from things we may not understand. (We will delve more into this topic in the next chapter.)

# PAGANISM AND SYNCRETISM

**Babylon's Exiles**

Especially from a religious perspective, Babylon was a polytheistic, multifaceted city with numerous temples, religious rites, and key deities. Enter the strange, monotheistic newcomers from Judah—sticking out like sore thumbs with their single God and unusual rites and rituals.

**Today's Generation**

The 2020 US Religion Census reported "more than 370 religious bodies, over 350,000 congregations, and over 160 million adherents" in the United States.[52] While remaining the most-practiced religion in America, Christianity has declined in several key areas—most notably in the number of people who identify as "Christian" and the number of people who claim membership in a Christian church (Protestant and Catholic).[53] Though the total number of Christian congregations increased slightly (2.2 percent since 2010), many denominations have experienced a significant drop, while independent churches have grown in number.[54]

Sixty years ago it would have been inaccurate to compare the US with ancient Babylon in terms of religious expression. Postwar America was a land of spiritual development and church growth (both in the number of Christian churches being built and in the nation's return to church after World War II). As had been the case for more than 175 years (1776 until the late 1950s), Judeo-Christian values dominated every sphere of life in the US. It's almost hard to imagine that up until the late '60s and '70s, most businesses were closed on Sundays (not just Chick-fil-A) so employees could enjoy the Sabbath with their families. Joanne Beckman from the National Humanities Center noted:

> At midcentury, Americans streamed back to church in unprecedented numbers. The baby boom (those born between 1946 and

> 1964) had begun, and parents of the first baby boomers moved into the suburbs and filled the pews, establishing church and family as the twin pillars of security and respectability. Religious membership, church funding, institutional building, and traditional faith and practice all increased in the 1950s. At midcentury, things looked very good for Christian America.[55]

This religious boom—to go along with the population boom—lasted a decade and a half, slowing during the tumultuous 1960s with civil rights unrest, the Vietnam War, campus protests, and the assassinations of the Kennedys and Martin Luther King Jr. In the aftermath, the late '60s and early '70s saw the Jesus Movement swell churches, and it looked as if Christianity was making a major comeback. But sadly, the increase was short-lived, and from the late 1970s until September 11, 2001, church attendance once again declined steadily.

There was a short-lived surge of attendance after 9/11, but then the decline resumed and continued for twenty years. Gallup's 2020 study of religion in America marked the first time in eight decades (i.e., since the study began) that church membership had fallen below 50 percent.[56] The most recent study from the Barna Group, which we discussed earlier, is the first real sign of major spiritual renewal in this nation in nearly sixty years.

Added to this rise in none-ism (no religious affiliation) is the phenomenon of syncretism. *Merriam-Webster* defines it like this:

> **syncretism-noun**
> syn·cre·tism 'siŋ-krə-ˌti-zəm
> **1 :** the combination of different forms of belief or practice
> **2 :** the fusion of two or more originally different inflectional forms[57]

For the Church we see spiritual syncretism everywhere we look. When a pop star talks about how they pray backstage before a show, what do they mean? In other words, to whom—or what—are they praying? When a friend says they are a Christian but they believe the resurrection is simply part of "the Jesus myth," how do we respond? When a friend tells us they are reading a book by a Christian author who believes all faiths lead to heaven, what do we think?

**For the Church, we see spiritual syncretism everywhere we look.**

This is what I mean when I talk about cultural Christianity, which is a form of syncretism along with nationalism and secular humanism. This isn't only for non-Christians but also for Christians who love the culture of Christianity and the culture of church but serve only for their own benefit.

This is also called moralistic therapeutic deism, a term used to describe the common but shallow belief system prevalent among teenagers and young adults in the US. It's not an official religion but a mindset that goes like this:

- A God exists who created and orders the world and watches over human life on earth.
- God wants people to be good, nice, and fair to each other, as taught in the Bible and by most world religions.
- The central goal in life is to be happy and feel good about oneself.
- God does not need to be particularly involved in one's life except when God is needed to resolve a problem.
- Good people go to heaven when they die.[58]

Coined by sociologists Christian Smith and Melinda Lundquist Denton, moralistic therapeutic deism is the idea that God is like a distant coach or therapist who wants you to be kind and happy but doesn't ask much from you unless you're in trouble. It's a form of *syncretism* because it *blends elements of traditional Christianity with secular, therapeutic culture and popular moral values*—often diluting or replacing core biblical truths in the process.

| BIBLICAL CHRISTIANITY | MORALISTIC THERAPEUTIC DEISM |
|---|---|
| God is sovereign, personal, holy, and involved. | God is distant and mostly uninvolved unless needed. |
| The Gospel is about sin, salvation, and surrender to Christ. | The goal is to feel good, be nice, and go to heaven. |
| Christianity calls for obedience, discipleship, and mission. | Faith is about being moral, feeling affirmed, and being happy. |
| Jesus is central. | Jesus is often optional or reduced to a life coach. |

**Similarities**

In the line of the Davidic kings, we see syncretism very clearly through Israelite rulers who prayed to Baal, sacrificed to Moloch, and placed pagan altars on the high places. King Saul consulted witches, and Ahab married the sorceress Jezebel. Syncretism was also alive and well in ancient Babylon, though a remnant of the exiled Jews did not worship or bow down to their foreign gods or idols. Today, we risk idolizing our Christian culture more than loving those who are not part of it or who do not speak our "spiritual dialect." It's critical that we break out of our centralized, church-building-based mindset to embrace those who neither understand it nor live in it.

## THE SPIRIT MOVES IN BABYLON

With the preceding comparison and context in mind, I want to examine how the faithful exiles—the ones who chose to honor the Lord's command to "seek the peace and prosperity of the city"—laid the groundwork for a major breakthrough in Babylon, as well as the Jews' return to Judah.

For instance, what truly distinguished the prophet Daniel was his wisdom and spiritual depth. Even in the pagan culture of the day, his Babylonian peers saw the power of God in Daniel and told the king, "There is a man in your kingdom in whom is the Spirit of the Holy God" (Daniel 5:11, NKJV).

Interestingly, in the Tanakh (the Hebrew Bible), the book of Daniel is not placed with the books of the Prophets (as it is in our Christian Bible). Instead, it's placed along with Esther in the Writings among the non-prophetic books. That's because, unlike Isaiah, Jeremiah, and Zechariah, God does not speak audibly to Daniel. Instead, Daniel hears directly from the *Spirit* of the Holy God through dreams and visions. And of course, the name of God is not found anywhere in the book of Esther. Both figures play key roles as heroes among pagans—as "strangers in a strange land" (see Exodus 2:22, NKJV) who hear through the Spirit. The Messianic Prophecy Bible Project tells us,

> While prophets also had the Ruach (Spirit) of God with them, the sages say that God's Spirit gave Daniel a depth of insight and revelation uncommon to prophets. . . . In this way, Daniel is considered to be a sage. And in the Talmud we read that "a sage is superior to a prophet" (Bava Batra 12a).[59]

In our similarly pagan culture we need to tune our ears to hear directly from the Holy Spirit. We also need to train up the younger generations to be attuned to the Holy Spirit—not just to hear from Him through us but to hear from Him *directly*. (More on this in chapter 8.)

Spirit-led discernment is especially critical in a time when Christianity is increasingly seen as a fringe religion—at best, misunderstood by many; at worst, hated by some. I can only imagine the swirl of teachings and philosophies the exiles were exposed to—a few of them good, most of them bad. But rather than ignore or avoid the culture, the Jewish remnant became students of it. In fact, to Daniel and his friends, "God gave knowledge and understanding of all kinds of literature and learning" (Daniel 1:17).

■ ■

**Spirit-led discernment is especially critical in a time when Christianity is increasingly seen as a fringe religion.**

■ ■

Daniel's public ministry began as he interpreted the dreams and visions of other men (Daniel 2–5). Then Daniel received his own prophetic visions (Daniel 7–12), including those about the future Messiah's victory. Jesus Himself quotes Daniel's end-time prophecies in Matthew 24:15 and Mark 13:14.[60]

The only way for a person to survive spiritually in a climate like ancient Babylon was to hear from the Holy Spirit and cultivate intimacy with God. Daniel maintained his connection with the Spirit through a regimen of daily prayer. He was consistent in his time with the Lord, turning toward Jerusalem and praying three times a day (see Daniel 6:10–11, 13).

The incident with the lions' den happened late in Daniel's life. By that point, he had established himself with King Darius, who became the benefactor of Daniel's sage wisdom and gift of interpreting dreams. Again, we can learn from Daniel, as he remained committed to the Lord even while serving a king who did not share his faith. We are often called to serve those who do not share—or even respect—our beliefs and to minister to the next generations who are increasingly suspicious of organized religion. I would offer that the only way to do so is to remain surrendered to and guided by the Holy Spirit—just as Daniel was.

## AUTHENTICITY SPURS ADAPTATION

The witness of the faithful exiled remnant reminds me of the popular adage "You can't give away what you don't have." In other words, the Jews weren't pretending or posturing to gain favor with the powers that be. They spoke the language, knew the customs, and understood the culture, but they were also "the real deal"—they understood and interpreted the times in a way that did not compromise or water down their beliefs.

Their faith had big, sharp incisors; they were lions of Judah with spiritual teeth that sank deep into the culture they were sent to evangelize. Their authentic faith, tested in fire and fanned by the Spirit, left indelible marks and gained them great favor in a pagan world. So too will ours when we let it loose.

The faithful exiles are a powerful prototype for us today of how to stand strong in God's truth while interpreting the culture and understanding how the younger generations act and think. It's like developing a great translation of a foreign novel, such as Tolstoy's *War and Peace*: The more we stick to the original source material and accurately convey the author's voice, the more effective the translation will be.

Just as it would be ridiculous to ask Americans to learn Russian in order to read Tolstoy, we must abandon our attempts to force outdated and antiquated methods of evangelism and discipleship on the next generations. As the old saying goes, "You can lead a horse to water, but you can't make it drink." Similarly, the faithful exiles accurately translated the culture and mastered it, both for God's glory and the future liberation of their people.

Notice, however, that this was a long process, and their character was bathed in God's Spirit and cultivated over a lifetime. And for their faith, their lives were endangered. In a royal setup those jealous of Daniel's favor with Darius tricked the king into issuing a thirty-day decree that forbade anyone from praying to any god or man except the king himself. Daniel defied the decree and continued to pray to God three times a day, and for his faithfulness he was arrested and condemned to the lions' den.

God doesn't withhold His favor from the faithful. Though he should have been torn to shreds, Daniel was miraculously protected because the Lord "shut the mouths of the lions" (Daniel 6:22). When Darius realized he'd been deceived, he ordered all the conspirators and their families to be thrown into the lions' den. Daniel 6:24 records, "And before they reached the floor of the den, the lions overpowered them and crushed all their bones." It's an amazing story of justice prevailing in the face of opposition. The same, of course, can be said of Daniel's friends Shadrach, Meshach, and Abednego, who survived the fiery furnace (see Daniel 3:8–25).

**God doesn't withhold His favor from the faithful.**

The entire experience of Daniel braving the lions' den had a profound impact on Darius, who wrote a decree that the entire kingdom was to revere the God of the exiles—the One who "rescued Daniel from the power of the lions" (Daniel 6:26–27).

This is a powerful and tangible example of how God loves to move through His children—the faithful remnant who stand strong in Him, even in the face of antagonism. It's also a powerful reminder that as we work with and among the younger generations, we must not hold back or water down the message of the cross. Like a lion, we don't have to defend it or blunt its bite but simply let it loose to sink deeply into the culture.

The exiles are the main characters in a story of prophetic reversal: What the enemy intended for bad, God intended for good. Two hundred years later we see the same type of prophetic reversal take place through Esther, as God used her to save the Jewish people from Haman's plan to annihilate them.

These acts of God moving in the midst of pagan culture should give us hope that as we minister in this current climate, He will always be faithful to walk beside us. In the next chapter we will look at methods and approaches for discipleship among Generations Z and Alpha.

The Lord gave this word to Jeremiah regarding the young remnant:

> My eyes will watch over them for their good, and I will bring them back to this land. I will build them up and not tear them down; I will plant them and not uproot them. I will give them a heart to know me, that I am the LORD. They will be my people, and I will be their God, for they will return to me with all their heart.
>
> —Jeremiah 24:6–8

We can take the words of this prophecy and apply them to our current situation: The Lord is watching over the younger generations, and He is bringing them back to Him. He will build them up and not tear them down; He will plant them and not uproot them. He will give them a heart to know Him—that He is the Lord. They will be His people. He is giving them a heart to know Him, and He is their Lord!

# PART III

# WHERE WE ARE GOING

# CHAPTER 8

# Discipling the Future

What does discipleship look like a quarter of the way into the first century of a freshly minted millennium? As with all things, we start with Jesus. Three of His directives tell us:

1] "And whoever does not carry their cross and follow me cannot be my disciple" (Luke 14:27).

2] "Take my yoke upon you and learn from me, for I am gentle and humble in heart, and you will find rest for your souls. For my yoke is easy and my burden is light" (Matthew 11:29–30).

3] "Therefore go and make disciples of all nations, baptizing them in the name of the Father and of the Son and of the Holy Spirit, and teaching them to obey everything I have commanded you. And surely I am with you always, to the very end of the age" (Matthew 28:19–20).

Stripped down to its simplest definition, discipleship is becoming more like Christ. To be a follower of Christ is to take up the work of the Kingdom and carry one's cross. And by doing so, we put on Jesus' yoke—His redemptive mission—and take His message to the geographical, digital, and generational corners of the earth.

The good news is that the Good News never changes. It was the same in the beginning, when "the Word was with God" (John 1:1); it was the same when the exiles were trafficked into Babylon; it was the same when Jesus rose from the dead and ascended to heaven; and it is the same today. The spiritual foundations of discipleship are no different for Generations Z and Alpha, and they will not have changed in another millennium, if Jesus should tarry.

■ ■

**The spiritual foundations of discipleship are no different for Generations Z and Alpha.**

■ ■

If truth is indeed a lion, needing no defense but only to be set free, then our approach to discipling the younger generations must also be based in the timeless truths of the Gospel. No punches pulled, no holds barred—but in a language they understand. Message over methods, but adaptive methods nonetheless.

## IT'S ALL ABOUT THE *IMAGO DEI*

There's no huge mystery or secret formula for discipling anyone at any age at any time. It all comes down to what Paul tells us in his letter to the Corinthian church:

> And we all, who with unveiled faces contemplate the Lord's glory, are being transformed into his image with ever-increasing glory, which comes from the Lord, who is the Spirit.
>
> —2 Corinthians 3:18

It's always about transformation into the *imago Dei*—the image of God—through the power and direction of the Holy Spirit. Discipleship is about believers in Christ walking together, learning from one another, supporting one another, and growing in their Spirit-driven image transformation process.

Jesus told us what the output looks like: "If you hold to my teaching, you are really my disciples. Then you will know the truth, and the truth will set you free" (John 8:31–32). It doesn't matter if you are an eighty-five-year-old member of the Silent Generation raised at the end of the Industrial Age or a ten-year-old Gen Alpha preteen born into the Adaptive Age. It's the same process.

What differs, however, is how we all view the redemption process—our frame of reference. The *what*, *why*, and *who* remain the same: atonement, redemption, Jesus. It's the *how* and *where* that change.

The beauty is that the ground is flat at the foot of the cross. No matter our age, generation, culture, or background, we all stand before the cross the same way: through repentance into redemption. We may approach from different routes and pathways, but we all end up standing before the cross and its offer of redemption.

## SEVEN MAJOR SHIFTS: INSIDE THE MIND OF GENERATIONS Z AND ALPHA

The question, then, isn't *what* we are bringing to the younger generations but *how* we are bringing it. Building on the characteristics that make Gen Z and Alpha tick, which we covered in earlier chapters, I want to explore seven key shifts that have taken place between Baby Boomers/Generation X and the younger generations (Gen Z and Gen Alpha).

1] **Confidence is morphing into caution.** All the confidence and swagger that Boomers and Gen Xers had is morphing into caution with Millennials, Gen Z, and even Gen Alpha because of the age of disruption these younger generations live in. And because that confidence isn't there on a large scale, we have to answer their young, cautious hearts as we propel them forward in the call of God for their lives.

Many of us were raised in a time when the Church touted *size* and *quality* as key attractants (e.g., size of the worship center and quality of the sermons). For today's prefigurative thinkers (i.e., the speed of change means young people are acquiring life skills from places other than their elders), those factors are not as important. The younger generations are looking for access, engagement, and community—for people to help them navigate the changes flying at them. They're looking for churches that have an access point built for them, content that's engaging, and a community to fulfill their purpose alongside.

**The younger generations are looking for access, engagement, and community.**

Our job is to open multiple doorways through which Gen Z and Alpha can have these needs met. This doesn't necessarily mean they need a ton of *program* options (task-heavy and potentially expensive), but they're looking for *opportunity* options: an open door—and people available—to ask questions and get answers; events where they can gather with their peers in a comfortable, safe atmosphere; and resources and tools for them to grow in Christ under teachers and leaders who speak their language.

2] **Idealism is morphing into pragmatism.** Idealism existed in previous generations about the perfect home, the perfect job, the perfect family, 2.5 kids, the white picket fence, and so on. But now that idealism is morphing into pragmatism. The next generations aren't saying, "Give me a dream." They're saying, "Tell me how to build and live out my dream."

3] **Attaining an education is morphing into hacking one.** The quicker you can get the education to get to the calling and purpose you feel you're designed for, the better. Too often we make people jump through hoops to get to something, rather than just paving the way for them and making it easy. Young people who are hungry to be spiritually educated aren't looking to jump through hoops. They're asking you to make an open way for them, build the structures around them, and give them the necessary foundations quickly so they can continue to grow in Christ.

You may be thinking that Gen Z and Alpha sound like self-serving generations, but keep in mind that the technologies created by Boomers, Gen Xers, and Millennials have shaped this expectation. Advances in technology have seen tech adapt to our needs, online education being only one of them. Further, many of today's educational models are built to meet the needs of generations past. This alone demands a restructure of educational attainment and development.

4] **Spending money is morphing into saving money.** We see it today with disruptions in economies all over the world. A

January 2025 poll by Talker Research revealed that Gen Z saves more money than any other generation polled:

> 21 percent of Generation Z (people born between 1997 and 2012) save between 1 and 10 percent, and 25 percent save between 11 and 20 percent each month. In addition, 12 percent of Gen Zers manage to save around 21 to 30 percent of their monthly wage. . . . [In comparison,] 32 percent of Baby Boomers (people born between 1946 and 1964) don't save money. Additionally, 33 percent of Generation X (those born between 1965 and 1980) don't save any money. [61]

Young people are watching the cost of living skyrocket, and they are concerned, cautious, and realistic.

5] **Consuming media is morphing into creating or publishing media.** Not only do we want to take it in, but we also want to be the authors of everything we produce. This is one of the drivers of Web3, the new iteration of the internet, which we will discuss in the next chapter. The gist is that a decentralized internet is evolving in which people will have more control over what they create and how they create and share it.

6] **Viral messages are morphing into vanishing messages.** In the digital (virtual) world, you can curate and control a preferred narrative. And in that world you can always start over—a phenomenon that can rewire a person's brain to believe that starting over is always an option. The problem, of course, is that this is not how the real world works.

As we pursue discipleship with the younger generations, it's important for us to know that they expect to be able to start over and have no consequences for their mistakes because they're wired to do that online. We need to guide them in the journey of not only repentance but also understanding the weight of repentance and the weight of forgiveness. Yes, all your sins are washed away, but that doesn't mean you get to repeat them over and over again.

7] **Text messaging is morphing into iconic messaging.** The old saying "A picture is worth a thousand words" could not be more accurate in this posttruth era. We are living in a time where emotions are captured more than information and feelings trump facts. We see it with memes; we see it with posts and shares on social media; we see it with reels and videos. I can provide information all day when it comes to the Word of God, but if I am not bringing young people into the narrative and revealing the heart of God in everything I say, write, and otherwise deliver, I am robbing them of the opportunity to process that information in the way they understand.

***

These seven shifts all point to one thing: the end of the Information Age and the advent of the Adaptive Age, where one's value isn't based on what they know but on how well they adapt that knowledge. Understanding this, in light of the seven shifts, points to the need for a new adaptive approach to discipleship.

## DISCIPLESHIP THROUGH THE AGES

While the *why* and *who* of discipleship are eternal, our focus shifts to the *how*. With the four ages in mind (as detailed in chapter 3), we can filter discipleship the following ways:

1] ***Imago Dei (Image of God)*—Agricultural Age (Adam–1750)** You will recall that in the Agricultural Age, the question of value was, "Who are you?" A key metric in the social fabric was who your parents and ancestors were. From a Kingdom standpoint this points us to the *imago Dei* and *who we are* in light of God's image. Many discipleship models of that day focused on the *imago Dei* reflected in the life of the disciple.

2] ***Missio Dei (Mission of God)*—Industrial Age (1750–1950)** The Industrial Age shifted value from identity to function, asking, "What do you do?" In that sense, the *missio Dei* became a primary focus in terms of what you do for God in accomplishing His redemptive mission within the context of your life. This was the great period of missional work, not only in places like Asia, Africa, South America, and India but also evangelistically on a local level. As a result, the discipleship emphasis shifted to the disciple realizing their calling and purpose.

3] ***Cogitatio Dei (Thinking like God)*—Information Age (1950–2022)** A key social value asked in the Information Age was, "What do you think?" In an age where value was ascribed based on what you knew and how well you could contribute what you knew, it's no wonder that the major discipleship focus was on having the mind of Christ and thinking like Him. Apologetics, renewed interest in theological study, and even missional study emerged as disciples longed to understand how to work out their calling to have the mind of Christ. The *cogitatio Dei* is absolutely key in an age of defending your faith.

4] ***Motus Dei (Moving like God)*—Adaptive Age (2022–?)** In 2022 the Information Age drew to an end and the Adaptive Age emerged. Think of adaptive technologies like AI, Web3, and the metaverse. Not only will the youngest generations on the planet grow up in a technologically adaptive world, but they will also be valued on how well they adapt what they know to the world around them—how well they move. In such a climate, it's essential that the discipleship emphasis be on helping the next generation learn how to adapt the mission of God across diverse contexts. In short, they need to "move like God." In the Adaptive Age the emphasis is on the *motus Dei*, or "how to move like God moves."

## DISCIPLESHIP IN THE ADAPTIVE AGE

The Adaptive Age in which these young people are living encourages fluidity and self-definition through digital means. In one sense the "What do you think?" paradigm encourages freedom of expression and individuality, but in a spiritual sense this can also lead to identity formation disconnected from the *imago Dei.* If we elevate the importance and value of our own thoughts over God's thoughts, we enter dangerous waters. The Church must counter this by anchoring a young person's identity in the unchanging truth that they are created in God's image and sustained there through the *cogitatio Dei.* That is how they can then move adeptly and deftly in the *motus Dei.*

■ ■

**If we elevate the importance and value of our own thoughts over God's thoughts, we enter dangerous waters.**

■ ■

The first step is spiritual formation rooted in the doctrine of the *imago Dei*, emphasizing that a person's value and worth are found in their creation by God, not in cultural labels or personal achievements. The focus here is on teaching individuals their inherent value as image bearers of God, articulated as the *imago Dei* in Genesis:

> So God created mankind in his own image, in the image of God he created them; male and female he created them.
>
> —Genesis 1:27

The core of spiritual formation revolves around understanding who we are in Christ, our connection to creation, and our place within God's ordered world. We must shift our thinking toward discipleship programs that meet today's younger generations where they live and think. Discipleship practices should emphasize spiritual formation that reinforces identity in Christ rather than shifting cultural values or technological trends. Small groups, mentoring, and community-building efforts should focus on helping young people explore their identity as beloved children of God.

As Generation Alpha enters the workforce, the traditional idea of working to fit into an established system is no longer viable. Instead, we have exited the Industrial and Information mindsets and entered the Adaptive paradigm, where adaptation is more important than traditional knowledge and skill sets.

Put another way, the speed at which a person can successfully adapt to a new technology or digital trend trumps traditionalism. Earned your four-year degree in computer science? Too bad—almost everything you learned four years ago is obsolete. Can you morph, curate, or reinvent different skills to keep up and adapt? That's the question Generations Z and Alpha now confront in their college career centers and in the workforce.

In her incisive article "How to Win in the New Economy," Adaptive Age entrepreneur and generalist Milly Tamati writes,

> We're entering a new economy. One that nobody is talking about, and very few are prepared for. . . . We quietly entered The Adaptive Economy in 2022. Here's how I know:
>
> - 65% of young people will do jobs that don't exist yet.
> - Today, more than half of LinkedIn members hold jobs that stand to be disrupted or augmented by AI (. . . and FYI LinkedIn has 1billion+ users).
> - The average half-life of skills is now less than five years, and in some tech fields it's as low as two and a half years. For millions of workers, upskilling alone won't be enough. We need to prepare workers to deal with whatever comes down the line, versus upskilling them with specific skills.
>
> So, quick math. The average half-life of skills is now less than five years. If a degree takes 4-6 years, and practical work experience takes another 4-6 years, well, the math ain't mathing. . . . You'll reach redundancy before you reach mastery.[62]

This is where the Adaptive Age natives—Gens Z, Alpha, Beta—will live and work. Tamati refers to "spiky careerists" and explains their function:

> Spiky careerists cross sectors, industries, domains, and roles. They are not constrained by traditional boxes. They make horizontal, vertical, and diagonal career moves. If they were a piece on a chessboard, they would be the queen. Powerful, because she knows she can move as far as necessary, in any direction.[63]

If workers in the Industrial and Information Ages were specialists who learned a specific skill, such as accounting, and practiced it for forty years, those in the new Adaptive Age will be generalists—compelled to move in multiple directions through multiple jobs requiring multiple sets of skills.

In the broader context, younger generations must discern their mission in a world where adaptability and innovation are prized. The rise of the adaptive economy means that many traditional jobs will disappear, and Gen Alpha will need to navigate careers that do not yet exist. In this context, the Church's role is to help them discover God's mission for their lives, regardless of changing career paths. The Church must learn to be nimble and flexible, willing to adapt methods that make the greatest impact and abandon those that no longer work for today's digitally driven generations.

**Younger generations must discern their mission in a world where adaptability and innovation are prized.**

Vocational discipleship will help Generations Z, Alpha, and Beta connect their skills and talents to God's broader mission, empowering them to live out their faith in nontraditional career paths, gig economies, and digital spaces. Local churches must explore ways to integrate practical vocational training with spiritual development, preparing students to thrive in the marketplace while fulfilling their divine purpose.

In this context the Church's role is to help individuals discover their calling and purpose—to understand the *missio Dei* for their lives. In Ephesians 2:10 the apostle Paul writes that we are "created in Christ Jesus to do good works." Discipleship means preparing believers for service and work that align with God's mission.

## ACCESS, ENGAGEMENT, COMMUNITY, AND TRANSACTION

The Industrial Age valued production, performance, and quantity, but the Information and now Adaptive Ages value access, engagement, and community. For example, in 2023, Gallup reported that young people spend more than 4.8 hours per day scrolling through their social media platforms, which neurologically rewires how they process information.[64]

Access, in this case, means whether something is easily accessible, be it an app, a podcast, or even news. Next, it must be engaging. If a post on social media doesn't engage a young person within three seconds, they keep scrolling. Finally, it must have community surrounding it. Young people ask themselves, perhaps subconsciously, "Are there others who agree with this?" Access. Engagement. Community. Then comes transaction—is this engagement transactional?

Here's the problem when it comes to the Church's role and responsibility: For the most part, local churches are designed to reach consumers, but we really need to reach publishers. Put another way, the Church is built to reach an Industrial Age generation that faded away more than half a century ago. I'll prove it.

In the same way the Industrial Age valued production, performance, and quantity, the Church still does—perhaps even more so. We judge a church on its service production value, how well the worship team and preacher perform, and how many people are in the seats. All of those metrics are Industrial Age markers.

But today's generations simply don't care as much about church size, production values, or performance. Instead, they are asking questions about access, engagement, and community, and whether something is transactional. They want to know:

- Is there an *access* point for someone like me to be a part of this?
- Am I being *engaged*, and is this church actually answering the questions I'm asking?
- Is there a *community* that believes in what I'm seeking, and can I be a part of that community?

**Today's generations simply don't care as much about church size, production values, or performance.**

## TEACHING TRUTH IN A POSTTRUTH ERA

It's no secret that we've left the Judeo-Christian era in America far behind. With the advent of the Sexual Revolution in the 1960s, our nation entered a postmodern era, followed by the current era in which we find ourselves: the posttruth (and post-Christian) era. In posttruth America, one's feelings and thoughts are more valued than facts.

In an era where misinformation, competing ideologies, and relativism dominate public discourse, the younger generations must learn how to think biblically. Developing the mind of Christ will enable them to critically engage with culture without losing sight of God's truth. If we stay on our current course, we run the risk of becoming what many nations in Europe have become: pre-Christian. This means that a culture has become so post-Christian that, in the once-Christianized nation, no one even knows about Jesus.

In this transition period from the Information to Adaptive Age, we must teach students to evaluate the overwhelming amount of content they encounter and process it biblically. This involves theological discussions and apologetics training to help them authentically contend with the world while maintaining a biblical worldview. The Church's focus during this time must be on helping believers develop the mind of Christ, with Philippians 2:5 as a guiding verse: "In your relationships with one another, have the same mindset as Christ Jesus."

Discipleship also needs to include training in cultural discernment and critical thinking that aligns with the teachings of Scripture. The Church must focus on developing pathways that emphasize biblical literacy and cultural discernment—twin load-bearing walls in the structure of the future Church. This can be achieved through apologetics, theological discussions, and cultural engagement strategies that emphasize discernment and wisdom in decision-making.

In addition, the Church must prepare Generations Z and Alpha for a world where traditional education systems fail to prepare them for future work. They need to learn how to adapt spiritually and navigate their personal callings while engaging with the rapid pace of societal and technological change.

Young people today are being hired right after graduation, not for how much they know but for how well they can adapt what they know to ever-changing contexts. We need to be able to step in with the guidance of the Holy Spirit—to move with God and stay on mission with fluidity and an open mind. God is challenging us to work with this generation and not be so rigid about how His mission is fulfilled. Rather, He calls us to consider how the Holy Spirit might want to accomplish His mission through us, the generations working together.

Discipleship for Generations Z and Alpha must include mission-focused training that teaches the younger generations how to engage and redeem culture. This could include digital evangelism, biblical justice initiatives, and marketplace ministries empowered to bring biblical values into every aspect of life.

## ADAPTIVE AGE TRANSFORMATION

In the Adaptive Age, where change is constant, the greatest skill the younger generations can develop is the ability to move and adapt while staying rooted in Christ. It is not enough to know the truth; they must be able to apply it flexibly in varying contexts and rapidly shifting cultural landscapes. This includes digital spaces, AI-influenced environments, and evolving social contexts. We must equip students to recognize where God is at work in these areas and train them to join in His mission. Acts 17:28 is a capstone verse here: "For in him we live and move and have our being."

**We must equip students to recognize where God is at work in these areas and train them to join in His mission.**

*Motus Dei* emphasizes the dynamic nature of God's movement in history, culture, and technology, and discipleship should reflect this. In the Adaptive Age, the Church must disciple believers in how to move with God in a constantly shifting world. Romans 12:2 calls for the renewal of the mind, which becomes central as believers learn to adapt without compromising their faith, discerning where God is at work and joining Him in mission.

In this age of syncretism and relativism, it's also critical that we stress the importance of the *cogitatio Dei*—the biblical call to put on the mind of Christ in all we do and think. I believe the *cogitatio Dei* is one of the most overlooked and underutilized discipleship tools today. The younger generations live in a time when no single truth is seen as better than any other. "Owning one's truth" and other forms of relativistic thinking are rampant. We must equip them to think like Christ and understand their identity in Him.

As adaptive technologies emerge and become increasingly accessible, many kinds of "virtual truths" will emerge. Because technological syncretism will allow individuals to create their own virtual worlds and realities, it will be vitally important to anchor this generation to their unchanging identity in Christ and to help them walk in the *cogitatio Dei.*

*Imago Dei. Missio Dei. Cogitatio Dei. Motus Dei.* From the beginning, we have had the image of God, which is communicated through the mission of God and articulated through the mind of Christ as the Holy Spirit moves among us. Everything we do flows from being made in the image of God, and everything we teach must begin there.

## CHAPTER 9

# AI and the Adaptive Age

It's time to fully open the Pandora's box that is artificial intelligence and all that comes with it. The Adaptive Age, however, isn't just about AI, as we will explore.

I am neither a machine learning engineer nor a robotics expert. There is a dizzying amount of fascinating reading out there about how AI is revolutionizing our society. My goal isn't to provide an in-depth overview of artificial intelligence—its roots, shoots, and fruits—but to take a fifty-thousand-foot survey in the pursuit of our goal: equipping the saints to do the work of the Kingdom in the Adaptive Age that is now upon us.

Much of my early exposure to AI was through science fiction films such as *2001: A Space Odyssey* (with the quietly malevolent HAL), *Alien* and its sequels (with the creepy voice of Mother), the *Blade Runner* films (replicants), *I, Robot*, and *WALL·E* (a personal favorite). At the risk of stereotyping my fellow Gen Xers (and those older), the phrase *AI* can elicit slightly sinister or foreboding emotions for those of us born before 1990.

To set the foundation, here's a basic definition of artificial intelligence (AI), provided by NASA:

> Artificial intelligence refers to computer systems that can perform complex tasks normally done by human-reasoning, decision making, creating, etc.[65]

I'm not anti-AI by any stretch—I'm actually an early adopter—and I'd like to disabuse you of the notion that AI is anything but a tool that can be used either positively or negatively. Put in spiritual terms, just as the internet can be used for all sorts of evil *or* as a powerful evangelism tool, I believe AI is neither inherently good nor evil. But it has the *possibility* to be either—or both. It's like a hammer that can be used to build a house or be wielded as a murder weapon.

For the body of Christ, three realities are upon us:

1] AI is here, and it's not going away.
2] It's more than a novel technology; it is transforming society by changing how we communicate, learn, and process the world.
3] The Church has a window of opportunity—and a responsibility—to use AI as a Gospel delivery tool to help fulfill the Great Commission.

■ ■

**The Church has a window of opportunity—and a responsibility—to use AI as a Gospel delivery tool to help fulfill the Great Commission.**

■ ■

As we've examined in previous chapters, the Adaptive Age has introduced unprecedented cultural and technological shifts. Just as Babylon reshaped the Jews' worldview during the Exile, today's digital and AI-driven world is reshaping how the next generations perceive truth, identity, and community. The printing press was an epoch-shaping invention, and so was the internet—and now so is AI.

This is a disruption, not an interruption. As we move deeper into the Adaptive Age, ongoing disruptions in technology, society, and culture will continue to challenge how the Church operates and how it disciples the next generations. Forecasting these disruptions allows us to be proactive rather than reactive in shaping the future of ministry.

The changes at our doorstep are not just about AI—they're about interrelated phenomena that are the hallmarks of the Adaptive Age. I want to investigate ways these phenomena can be harnessed to empower leaders and ministries to navigate the rapidly changing cultural landscape with wisdom, faithfulness, and creativity. I can't overstate this: The goal is not simply to prepare the Church to survive the disruptions of the Adaptive Age but to help it *thrive, innovate, and lead* in a world that is increasingly complex and fluid.

## AI IN MINISTRY: THE UPSIDE

Here's a brief assignment: If you've never used an AI platform like ChatGPT, go check it out. It's easy to use—just type in a question, and see what comes out. For example, as I was writing this chapter, I typed in, "How will AI change the way Christians live?" In 11.46 seconds, the AI engine produced an informative 347-word article on the subject. It concluded with this pearl of wisdom: "AI won't necessarily change *what* Christians believe, but it will change *how* they live out those beliefs—how they worship, learn, connect, and witness in a digital world."[66]

So, yes, AI can be used as a very powerful tool for the Church. Here are just a few of the many ways it can be used:

- Apps for Bible study, devotionals, and commentaries
- Sermon research, preparation, and organization
- Church marketing research and analysis (understanding congregational needs, demographic insights, and outreach planning)
- Bible translation for global outreach with culturally contextualized messages tailored to specific nations and people groups

## AI: PROCEED WITH CAUTION AND DISCERNMENT

AI also presents challenges in discerning authenticity, protecting privacy, and maintaining relational depth. A recent Barna Group survey revealed concerns from pastors regarding the effects of AI on relationships:

> Nearly nine in 10 pastors (89%) feel AI will have at least some impact on relational quality, with over half of these pastors (56%) saying this impact will be negative. Conversely, U.S. adults are four times more likely than pastors to say they feel that the impact of AI on relationships will be positive (21% vs. 5%), and they're significantly less likely to say that they feel this impact will be negative (43% vs. 56%).[67]

Unsurprisingly, the younger the person, the more open they are to AI—they don't have the same aversions older Americans tend to have due to negative depictions in media and culture. It's time for a paradigm shift in God's body: Rather than taking a fortress mentality toward AI and other technologies, the Church must discover how to use these advancements for His Kingdom. Thankfully, the Barna survey also revealed, "Three in four U.S. pastors (77%) agree that God can work through AI."[68]

■ ■

**It's time for a paradigm shift in God's body.**

■ ■

I believe we have a five-to-seven-year window of opportunity for the Church to incorporate AI in areas such as administrative efficiency, discipleship, biblical literacy, continuing education and Bible learning, cultural discernment, and evangelism. We also need to balance these benefits with a theological critique of AI's potential to depersonalize ministry. Can an AI virtual counselor programmed for Christian responses really provide the help needed by a believer in crisis? Can an AI-manned suicide hotline replace a human responder?

Likewise, what are the ethical implications of what it means to be a Christian in the age of AI, especially in light of the *imago Dei*? As eternal creatures crafted and individually formed in the image of God, how shall we live with AI? Consider the theory of *deus ex machina*, which literally means "god from the machine" and refers to an improbable conclusion to an otherwise impossible situation.

Think of a situation where the person about to fall off a cliff is suddenly rescued by a helicopter. That only happens in the movies, right? But why? It's a contrived, unrealistic solution to a life-or-death problem. In the same way, it's improbable to believe that a man-made technology such as AI (no matter how sophisticated) will ever be able to conjure or mimic the Spirit of God. AI is spiritless—it literally has no spirit and, therefore, can never be an eternal creature. To truly reflect the Spirit of God, something would have to share in His eternal, life-giving, and personal nature—which no human invention ever can.

The upshot is that God will never be in the machine. The *imago Dei* comes from Him and resides in us, not in animatronics or robotics. No doubt, we need Holy Spirit-led guidance and answers to the question of how far AI can take us in our Kingdom mission goals.

Our guiding principle should always be *deus extra machina*—"God outside of the machine." Our job is to use AI to our advantage, not the other way around.

## "TOTO, WE'RE NOT IN WEB2 ANYMORE"

Gen Z was the first generation fully born into the internet age, and Generation Beta (those born starting in 2025) will be the first fully AI generation. For the rest of us, the learning curve is steep, fast, and unending. There's no question that AI is affecting Gen X and Millennials entering the global workforce or navigating their mid-career life stages.

Arguably, however, the generations facing the steepest learning curve in the AI-influenced economy will be Gen Z and Gen Alpha. They were educated with an Information Age mindset (i.e., "go to school for four years to prepare for a forty-year career"), but they now must shift abruptly to adapt to new technologies and demonstrate greater flexibility than ever. Obsolescence is a major challenge as these Z and Alpha-generation young adults enter college and the job market. They must adjust to an entirely new adaptive paradigm that they were neither born into nor educated for. (Remember, they are prefigurative thinkers born mostly to cofigurative and postfigurative parents.)

For NextGen leaders and laypeople, there's good news: The Church has an excellent opportunity to minister to these young people as they scramble to adapt to new AI-influenced realities in the job market and culture. The concept of felt need versus real need applies: By creating church doorways that offer such services as vocational counseling and training, relational events and spaces, and life skills tools, we can meet the felt needs of the generation. What college-age person would say no to career and vocational events at a local church where they can hack real-world skills and receive current job market training? That's meeting the *felt need* before meeting their *real need* for Jesus.

**We can meet the felt needs of the generation.**

## WEB3 AND DECENTRALIZATION

Everything in our daily lives changes based on technology—our behaviors, the rhythms of our days, and the way we access education. Even our work changes based on the type of internet we use. I refer us yet again to Mead's words: "I call this new style prefigurative because in this new culture it will be the child—and not the parent and grandparent—that represents what is to come."[69] With the Adaptive Age and its technologies (such as the evolving internet), prefigurative learners will grasp the information first, and the previous generations will learn from them.

Since the internet became a household tool starting in the mid-1990s, there have been three versions: Web1, Web2, and Web3. Let's explore them.

### Web1: The Information Internet (1990s–c. 2007)

Web1 was the first version of the internet, which became an accessible household tool just over thirty years ago. It was basically a digital library built for consumers—users shaped by the Industrial and Information Ages. From the Industrial Age until about twenty years ago, people were consumers, and the only thing they wanted to do was consume. So it makes sense that when Web1 came out, that's who it was built for.

The big winners of the Web1 era were AOL, Google, and Yahoo, because they created space for us to access information and knowledge.

### Web2: The Interactive Internet (2007–2025)

The second version of the internet is the one we're most saturated with today. No longer primarily for information, Web2 is driven by interaction. Not only do you have a place to find information, but now there are platforms where community takes place. Social engagement fundamentally changed because of Web2, especially in the ways we connect and build community. Texting, social media sites, and messaging all became significant forms of digital community.

The more powerful Web 2 gets, the more powerful our hardware becomes. The technology isn't driving the internet—the internet is driving tech. As Web2 has increased in power and speed, it has driven the market to create more powerful tech. Smartphones, smart devices (e.g., tablets, smartwatches, fitness trackers), smart televisions, and even smart homes have evolved because of the power of Web2. The smartphone was a tipping point invention that took our handheld phones from information-gathering devices to interactive engagement tools.

The big winners of the Web2 era were YouTube, Facebook, Google, and Amazon. This is where the internet began to disrupt culture, including how we "do church." It was no longer just about access *to* knowledge (Web1) but about interacting *with* that knowledge. And now we're interacting with that knowledge within a framework of community (Facebook, Instagram, X, etc.).

We went from being Industrial Age-influenced consumers in Web1 to publishers with Web2 because of the way it affected our behaviors. If you doubt its effect, just check your phone's internet usage. How much time did you spend on your phone yesterday? *Reviews.org* reported that in 2024, "the average American checked their phones 205 times a day (nearly once every five minutes they were awake)." That equated to "5 hours and 1 minute on their phone per day, which adds up to a whopping 2.5 months per year!"[70]

The same process that rewires your brain when you learn a new language also kicks in when you spend just fifteen minutes or more on a screen. That's because both activities tap into neuroplasticity—your brain's ability to reshape itself based on what you focus on and engage with. Over time, screen time trains your brain to think in certain ways, reinforcing new patterns of attention, behavior, and even belief.

So even if we don't all speak the same verbal language, many of us are starting to speak the same digital one—and it's happening on a global scale. While technology can be a powerful tool, especially for learning and connection, too much screen time—especially when it's unfiltered or constant—can reshape how we process the world, and not always for the better.[71]

Even though we don't all speak the same verbal language, we're all speaking the same digital language—it's happening globally.

This digital globalism, coupled with the power, speed, and connectivity of Web2, has allowed us to move beyond strict information gathering to information sharing and creating. Thus, Web2, as the interactive internet, cultivated within us the need to become publishers.

When something happens to you online that changes your in-person expectations and behaviors, that's digital transformation. So many people have experienced digital transformation that we now want to externalize what we've internalized. For example, we might connect with an online social media group that likes a particular film genre. We begin to interact, exchange knowledge, and connect on a social and emotional level with others in the group. In Web1, where such digital connections were less available, interaction was typically one-sided—we gathered information for its own sake. Now, in Web2, we're not only gathering information but also interacting with others about it and publishing our own experiences and impressions.

Many churches still operate in an Industrial Age-Web1-era mindset, assuming the average church attender is a consumer seeking knowledge. In fact, they are now digitally transformed consumers who are used to not only consuming but also publishing what they see and do. Yes, they are seeking knowledge (consuming and internalizing truth), but they also crave community and engagement (publishing and externalizing). Jesus' last words before His ascension were all about publishing what we, as sons and daughters of the King, have internalized: We receive the gift of salvation, grow in its grace and knowledge, and then take the message to the ends of the earth (see Matthew 28:19–20).

There's a major disconnect between today's Web2 culture and those of us still thinking and acting within Web1 paradigms. This is a critical distinction, especially when it comes to Generations Z, Alpha, and soon Beta. We're stuck in Web1 while Web2 has fully arrived and Web3 is already emerging!

We live in a digital Babel with a singular digital language. What will our response be? As we discussed in chapters 6 and 7, God doesn't want to take us out of Babylon. He wants to place us in the midst of the city and its syncretism—in the midst of the noise and chaos, just as He did with the faithful remnant of Judah.

**We live in a digital Babel with a singular digital language. What will our response be?**

### Web3: The Integrated Internet

I love the Church too much not to share what I've learned and experienced. My goal isn't to provide every answer but to bother everyone else with the things that bother me.

I believe that by everyone focusing on the same disruptions (with varied contextualization), together we can find better ways to meet the needs of the world around us with the Gospel. That must be our posture as we approach the evolving—and newest—form of the internet: Web3.

No longer just the information internet or interactive internet, Web3 is the *integrated* internet.

Do you ever work from home? If so, you integrate, which means "to form, coordinate, or blend into a functioning or unified whole."[72] Working remotely, you've taken the technological and digital tools available to you and externalized internal motivations and actions. That's both digital transformation *and* integration. You've been able to synthesize and optimize those same tech tools to perform your vocation from your home office or even the corner of your bedroom.

Over the next five to seven years, Web3 will become the dominant form of online experience. As it begins to saturate every corner of the market, people will effectively move from being consumers to publishers to full-fledged adapters and creators. Their desire will not only be to publish in every atmosphere but also to adapt to it and create their own reality. This is what Web3 offers in every virtual space.

At its core Web3 provides a decentralized space to do what you want on the internet. Consider your bank, which is a centralized place that you visit either online or in person. Facebook, Instagram, X, and

TikTok are all centralized Web2 platforms. But in Web3, you can pull away from a single space and create your own reality without the restrictions of a centralized virtual (or physical) institution or location.

Keeping with the financial analogy, cryptocurrency is to Web3 what your banking app is to Web2. A cryptocurrency isn't run by a bank, however, but by people who use blockchain technology along with a trust market. For those new to the concept of blockchain, here is a brief introduction from IBM:

> Blockchain is a shared, immutable digital ledger, enabling the recording of transactions and the tracking of assets within a business network and providing a single source of truth. Blockchain operates as a decentralized distributed database, with data stored across multiple computers, making it resistant to tampering. Transactions are validated through a consensus mechanism, ensuring agreement across the network.[73]

We all need to get up to speed on decentralization, cryptocurrency, and blockchain dynamics because these concepts are already starting to play out in real time. For example, I have a friend in Zimbabwe who realized the economy wasn't helping the people he was trying to reach. So he gathered local businesses and leaders, and together they created a partially decentralized micro-economy, detached from the main government. In other words, they built their own economic ecosystem—complete with its own currency—that is now up and running.

This micro-economy has built trust between vendors, businesses, and clients with its own currency, which has become more robust and valuable than the Zimbabwean dollar. That's blockchain in action. In my friend's case, they've created a decentralized model independent of the central government. In effect, this is a DAO—a decentralized autonomous organization. The startling message is that you don't need a central bank, just as you don't need a centralized social media platform to create what you want. Decentralization is going to be the force that defines jobs, work, and expectations.

So what happens when decentralization hits the Church? We saw the decentralized mindset post-COVID-19 when people said, "I'm tired of church. I'm just going to go back to having my own 'church' at home by watching a worship service online." That can be a bit shortsighted, of course, because it leaves out a key tenet of New Testament Christianity: the fellowship of believers meeting together (see Acts 2:42).

Of course, it's not quite that simple, is it? That perspective lacks an exegetical understanding of the book of Acts. I don't believe "decentralized and autonomous" is necessarily what we need. People say, "We can just meet among ourselves; we don't need a church," but the Church doesn't need DAOs. It's not autonomous—it's knit together interdependently. We need *decentralized* and *integrated*, where we may be divorced from an overarching physical space, but we are still going to be the Church—with biblical leadership and order—in new spaces. This is called a DIO (decentralized integrated organization).

**We are still going to be the Church—with biblical leadership and order—in new spaces.**

Mind you, this is just the on-ramp to the twelve-lane superhighway that is Web3. Close study and observation will be needed for the Church to remain nimble, fluid, and adaptable with our methods and responses, especially for the native Adaptive Age generations (younger Gen Zs, Alphas, and Betas) who will only know Web3.

## VIRTUAL REALITY AND TRIBALISM

With Web3 we won't need centralized platforms for community (e.g., Instagram). Instead, we will create spaces to build our own reality and then invite others into that space. Think digital villages that our tribes will inhabit.

Decentralization has its benefits, but the risks here are real. We will no longer need to log in to our social media accounts to be invaded by every kind of syncretistic belief system. Instead, as young people build their virtual worlds and spaces, secular humanism will invade those spaces.

It calls us as believers to stand up, take note, and commit ourselves to equipping and training our youth in biblical and cultural discernment tactics and skills. It's apologetics—helping them to know what they believe, believe what they know, and articulate it in culturally adept ways.

In essence, Adaptive Age apologetics is helping adapters consume the Word of God (internalization) and walk confidently in the truths of their faith in all these new Web3 spaces (externalization). That's digital *and* spiritual transformation. It means we will need to meet them in their Web3 environment and train them to think with the *imago Dei* as their compass.

Imagine being a fourteen-year-old Christian and putting on your VR gaming headset in the metaverse. In the metaverse, you can create your own reality. Let's say I have a "truth" that really doesn't line up with *the* truth, but I don't care—it's *my* truth, and I want to live my truth any way I want. The problem is that I expect the rest of the world to validate it. Instead of just saying it with a hashtag on social media, I can create a community in the metaverse.

Not only that, but now I can globally tribalize and create my own tribe around my version of truth, even though it's not God's eternal truth. As a young teenager, I may have some misguided thoughts about Jesus, but my digital tribe is going to affirm me.

That affirmation in the metaverse is going to be something that I now expect in person (this is digital transformation). And therein lies the rub. What happens when that person who already spends four to six hours a day on a screen translates that into their physical space? Web3 has created a neurological digital language. We all are being rewired the same way, and all of us expect the same things of our world globally.

Then the fourteen-year-old takes off her VR headset because somebody invites her to church—not in the metaverse but in the physical world. She walks in with her version of truth, even though it's not *the* truth, and she assumes this physical tribe will act like her digital tribe. Don't miss this: She's going to expect the pastor and the church to allow her to create her own spiritual reality even though it's not in line with the Word of God.

This scenario is not from a movie. It's happening, and Web3 is leading us into a jarring collision between biblical Christianity and cultural Christianity. Ironically, cultural Christianity can look quite attractive, can't it? That's the way Satan has always operated—with lies seasoned with a dash of truth. Holy Spirit-led discernment is the only way forward, and that's what we must lead with as we walk into the younger generations' spaces, teach God's Word, and show them how to walk in it, defend it, and transmit it.

Our responsibility in raising up the next generation is to help them take their cultural moments and filter them through the Word of God so that what comes out is Kingdom culture (redeemed culture). That is how we become salt and light to the world. Someone who isn't biblically grounded becomes a "cultural Christian." They might show up to your church, go to your events, lift their hands, and sing your songs. They might post about Jesus on social media, but the minute a culturally triggering moment happens, they falter and leave.

Instead of taking a cultural moment and filtering it through the Word of God, they take the Word of God and filter it through that cultural moment. Any truths from Scripture that don't hold up against culture get thrown out, and what remains is secular humanism—Christianity without Christ.

This relates to Generations Z, Alpha, and Beta, but it relates to the rest of us too. After all, cultural Christianity has been a thing for a while now. It's just going to get more intense in the Web3 era. Christians may look the same, act the same, and talk the same in your youth groups, kids' ministries, young adult communities, and internship programs. But the minute something triggers them culturally, the cultural Christians leave and burn everything down on their way out. In contrast, biblical Christians exegete the moment—they filter culture through the Word of God—and whatever holds up at the end is Kingdom culture (again, "redeemed culture").

**Biblical Christians exegete the moment.**

Our job today is to redeem culture and teach people how to be biblical Christians rather than cultural Christians. In the post-Christian and posttruth era, these communities must understand Christ's truth, and the Church must help frame up reality on the foundation of that truth. Generation Alpha—those twelve years old and under—are natives of this reality. They're not foreigners, immigrants, or exiles. They weren't born in "Jerusalem" (the Judeo-Christian era before the mid-'90s); no, they were born in digital Babylon.

Two things will happen in the Church once Web3 and adaptive tech (including AI) begin to permeate:

1] *Resistance.* Some will resist the change and hold to the old attractional paradigms as the "correct" way to do church and ministry. They will do what the Church always does when faced with something suspicious: attack it, ignore it, or try to control it. No matter what, some will resist—there's no avoiding it. But Jesus didn't come into the world to attack, ignore, or control culture. He came to *redeem* it.

2] *Redemption.* The question isn't how we resist this change but rather, how we redeem it. How do we move into spaces like the metaverse and, instead of marrying it, bring Christ's redemptive message?

## MOVING IN REDEMPTION AND TRUTH

In Jeremiah 29:4–7, God gives the Jews a very clear word that He is the One who exiled them and brought them into Babylon. He tells them to marry, have sons and daughters, and give them in marriage. They are to move into the heart of the city—not hide in its outskirts—and pray for the peace and prosperity of that place.

It's no different today. God still calls His people to move into the place where people reside. He calls us to the city—to our digital Babylon. We are not called to resist the pagans, the "nones," or the atheists; we are to be His agents of redemption.

For many people, including cultural Christians, the response will be assimilation with the culture and abandonment of God's mission. The posture will be, "I'm just going to embrace it and let it change me, and I'll attack those who question me." The Church's response, however, is all about redemption rather than condemnation. Why should we expect anything less than assimilation into the culture from those who have not learned how to walk in it with Christ?

We have to be redemptively present in the midst of the Web3 world, and we need fresh Shadrachs, Meshachs, and Abednegos. We need Daniels and Ezekiels, whose voices rise and speak biblical truth to the current context. Everyone must submit themselves to God, and we must ask the question, "How do we prosper as the body of Christ in the midst of the metaverse, in the midst of a complex, pagan, decentralized Web3 world?"

As we approach this new age that will inevitably impact the thinking and values of the next generation more than previous ages, let's ask ourselves how we should move into that place. How do we birth spiritual sons and daughters there, and how do we increase there? How do we pray for the peace and prosperity of that place? We must find the answer, because that's the only thing that's going to redeem it.

This is what we have to do today, five to seven years before market saturation takes place. We study, plan, and prepare. We equip ourselves in His Word and filter the cultural moment through it. This preparation will help us align our expectations and the behaviors we need in order to adapt.

I'd like to offer three tangible steps we can take as the Church to ensure we don't go over the edge or miss this window of opportunity before us.

1] ***Make discipleship truly discipleship.*** I believe much of what we call discipleship in the Church today is just enhanced relationships that we celebrate. We say, "Hey, if you want to be discipled, join one of our small groups." But who's leading that small group, and what's the win for that small group leader? The win isn't just to teach the Word of God and disciple the attendees but also to grow the small group and keep people coming back.

While there's nothing wrong with multiplication, what really matters is the output—the kind of disciples being multiplied. What's in danger of going by the wayside is the teaching of the deep, transformative Word of God, imparted within an accountable atmosphere. Let's be honest: Sometimes people throw out accountability when they want to retain numbers.

Here's a clean, clear measure when it comes to discipleship: You know you're doing it right when it breeds evangelism. One of the most unfortunate things the Church has done—and now NextGen ministries do it too—is to disconnect discipleship from evangelism. We often host different events for each, but in reality, truly good discipleship breeds evangelism.

If you're being discipled and invested in with the things of Christ, you shouldn't be able to shut up about God. Whatever you spend your life investing in, all you want to do is talk about it. If you love football and it's fantasy football season, you are talking to everybody who knows what the shape of a football is—you're talking their ear off. Why? Because you know the players, the history, the story, and the franchises. You can talk for *hours*. Why? Because you have invested yourself in football.

**If you're being discipled and invested in with the things of Christ, you shouldn't be able to shut up about God.**

If discipleship today is really *discipleship*, why isn't there a natural wave of evangelism taking place with people talking about Christ? Maybe it's because what we call discipleship isn't always discipleship. Maybe it's just celebrated relationship, often in the context of pooled ignorance. We must once again make discipleship truly about discipleship.

2] ***Increase biblical literacy.*** Here's a sobering reality: This is the generation that has the most access to the Word of God (and commentary on it), but it's also the most biblically illiterate generation in history. As the old proverb goes, familiarity breeds contempt. In our context, with the proliferation of knowledge, there comes a resistance to it. Many times we think of biblical literacy as being able to name most of the books of the Bible and its key characters, and perhaps we pick it up and read it a few days a week. But it's so much more than that.

We need to raise our definition of biblical literacy and ask ourselves (and others) the hard questions: *Do I know the meta-narrative of God? Do I know how the Old Testament confirms the New Testament and vice versa? Do I know how the prophets speak about Christ and how He is the fulfillment of those prophecies? And do I know how to apply the Bible to my life?* Our young people will not be salt and light in the culture unless we teach them how to be biblically literate within the context of discipleship.

3] ***Teach cultural discernment.*** We need to insert cultural discernment into everything we say and do. For example, when a cultural moment happens, like I mentioned earlier, the goal is for people to know they've been discipled and to have attained sufficient biblical literacy to take that cultural moment, process it through the Word of God, and run with redeemed culture.

If in every sermon we are not talking about a cultural moment and helping people biblically analyze and apply it, we are robbing them of being salt and light. Not far from where I live is where the George Floyd tragedy happened. Did you know there are people in the Twin Cities close to that place—pastors and church leaders—who have chosen not to talk about it? How can we be more culturally disconnected than that?

When such significant cultural disruptions take place, we need to know the Word of God well enough to apply it and help our churches analyze the cultural event in a way that leads them to be culturally redemptive. It's a travesty when we walk past these moments without acknowledging the fiery furnace as we pass it by. We pretend the lions' den isn't actually happening. We must become culturally present in order to be instruments of God's redemption.

If we are going to meet this Web3 train that's coming down the tracks, we're going to have to curb the disruption and be able to lead people into truth. We need to make discipleship *discipleship*, sow into biblical literacy, and inject cultural discernment into everything we do. If we do that, I believe we will be ready for the train when it arrives.

## THE FUTURE BELONGS TO THE WIND-BORN

Is the Church hungry to disciple and evangelize Generations Z, Alpha, and Beta? I know the answer, because as I speak and meet with fellow believers and leaders from all over the world, the response is an emphatic, "Yes!"

The challenge is before us: Adapt our methods of interacting with those under thirty by using preaching, teaching, discipleship, and evangelism methods that they understand and that bring true spiritual transformation in the midst of disruption.

For our part, we must show the generations how to "move like God"—the *motus Dei.* Scripture supports and even encourages this:

> The wind blows where it wishes, and you hear its sound, but you do not know where it comes from or where it goes. So it is with everyone who is born of the Spirit.
>
> —John 3:8, ESV

Jesus draws a powerful metaphor here between the unpredictability of the wind and the life of the Spirit-filled believer. Just as the wind cannot be confined, those born of the Spirit are led by a power and direction not dictated by human systems, expectations, or patterns.

**We must show the generations how to "move like God"—the *motus Dei*.**

This is a staggering claim when you pause long enough to hear it. Jesus is saying that those who are born of the Spirit cannot be explained by natural logic, institutional structure, or cultural conformity. They're animated by another rhythm—God's rhythm. Their decisions may not make sense to the boardroom, the algorithm, or even their closest peers, but they make perfect sense in the Kingdom. Why? Because they are not marching to the beat of predictability; they are moving in response to the breath of the Spirit.

They are unmapped but not lost. They are untamed but not unanchored. They are unorthodox but not unfaithful. They follow the movements of the Spirit—sometimes invisible, often misunderstood, yet always effective.

You can feel this in the stories of Scripture. Spirit-led people were rarely the "safe" ones. They were disruptive, inconvenient, and deeply rooted in God but wildly unpredictable to others:

- Abraham left without knowing where he was going (Hebrews 11:8).
- Moses walked back into Egypt with a shepherd's staff and a stutter (Exodus 4:10–20).

- Philip left a revival in Samaria to talk to one man on a desert road (Acts 8:26–40).
- Paul changed entire missionary routes because the Spirit said no (Acts 16:6–10).

Each in his own way lived in response to a Spirit who cannot be seen but can always be trusted.

The Spirit is not irrational. He's just *higher*. His logic is not broken—it's just heavenly (Isaiah 55:8–9). This doesn't mean the Spirit leads people to be chaotic or careless. Quite the opposite. Spirit-led people aren't untethered—they're just tethered to a different center of gravity.

The world says, "Build platforms." The Spirit says, "Wash feet."

The world says, "Establish certainty." The Spirit says, "Walk by faith."

The world says, "Scale fast." The Spirit says, "Grow deep."

And here's the beauty: What the Spirit leads us to will not always make us visible, but it will always make us valuable—to the Kingdom, to the mission, to the movement of God on the earth.

**What the Spirit leads us to will not always make us visible, but it will always make us valuable.**

If the Spirit moves like wind and those born of the Spirit are to move likewise, then the servant of God must cultivate a lifestyle of sensitivity.

- Sensitivity → Strategy. Strategy is essential, but it must be Spirit-submitted.
- Availability → Achievement. The Spirit often uses the most available, not the most accomplished.

- Obedience → Outcome. We're not called to manufacture results but to faithfully respond.

In a world chasing control, precision, and artificial certainty, the Church must recover its birthright to be a people of the Wind.

This is not just about being charismatic—it's about being Christ centered and Spirit animated, refusing to build monuments to yesterday's moves and instead moving with the cloud (Numbers 9:17–23). The future of the Church will not be built on those who are merely well positioned but on those who are Spirit positioned—unafraid to be misunderstood, unashamed to be moved, and unrelenting in their obedience to the One who sends the Wind.

When Paul was in Athens, he pointed the Athenians to the statue of their unknown god. He met the Stoics, Epicureans, and philosophers of arguably the most syncretistic city in the world right where they lived—among their gods. And *then* he preached Jesus to them (Acts 17:16–34).

Paul understood that the Gospel is fluid and takes the shape of any container it fills. He allowed the Spirit to drive him, and he became "all things to all people" because he knew what was at stake (1 Corinthians 9:22). The shape—the way the Church approaches the generations—may change, but the contents—the message of Jesus—remain pure.

I end with Paul's words, which I believe perfectly articulate the posture we take as we become all things to all people for the sake of Jesus' message.

> Though I am free and belong to no one, I have made myself a slave to everyone, to win as many as possible. To the Jews I became like a Jew, to win the Jews. To those under the law I became like one under the law (though I myself am not under the law), so as to win those under the law. To those not having the law I became like one not having the law (though I am not free from God's law but am

under Christ's law), so as to win those not having the law. To the weak I became weak, to win the weak. I have become all things to all people so that by all possible means I might save some. I do all this for the sake of the gospel, that I may share in its blessings.

—1 Corinthians 9:19–23

# Acknowledgments

First and foremost, I want to express my deepest gratitude to my wife, Christina. Your love and support, along with our shared global calling as a family, have been my greatest source of strength and inspiration.

I am deeply appreciative of Rob Ketterling, lead pastor of River Valley Church. Pastor, your support and trust have given me the freedom to pursue the vision God placed in my heart, both within River Valley and beyond.

I am profoundly grateful to Dr. Rob Hoskins and the entire OneHope community. Rob, your inclusion of me in the OneHope family has helped me form the language and structure for the vision God gave me. You've opened doors for me to connect with the global Church and gain a deeper understanding of its future.

I also extend my heartfelt thanks to Dr. Billy Wilson and the Empowered21 organization. Dr. Wilson, your dedication to the next generation and your leadership have created space for people like me to grow and thrive. Empowered21 has been a vital network, allowing me to engage with like-minded leaders from around the world.

To everyone at River Valley Church, OneHope, and Empowered21, and to all the readers and supporters of this journey, thank you for being part of this mission. Your encouragement and partnership have been invaluable.

# Endnotes


1. See Luke 19:1-10.
2. See John 4:1-26.
3. See Luke 8:26-39.
4. See Margaret Mead, *Culture and Commitment: A Study of the Generation Gap* (Natural History Press/Doubleday & Company, 1970), 72.
5. Margaret Mead, "Generational Ties," in *Youth: Divergent Perspectives*, ed. Peter Manning (John Wiley & Sons, 1973), 204.
6. PRRI, "Generation Z's Religiosity and Religious Affiliation" in *PRRI Generation Z Fact Sheet,* March 29, 2024, https://prri.org/spotlight/prri-generation-z-fact-sheet. Notably, these findings closely mirror the results of the 2021 American National Family Life Survey by the Survey Center on American Life. See https://www.americansurveycenter.org/download/2021-american-national-family-life-survey.
7. PPRI, "2022 PRRI Census of American Religion: Religious Affiliation Updates and Trends," February 24, 2023, https://prri.org/spotlight/prri-2022-american-values-atlas-religious-affiliation-updates-and-trends.
8. Pew Research Center, *Modeling the Future of Religion in America*, September 13, 2022, https://www.pewresearch.org/religion/2022/09/13/modeling-the-future-of-religion-in-america.
9. Geogory A Smith et al., "Decline of Christianity in the U.S. Has Slowed, May Have Leveled Off," Pew Research Center, February

26, 2025, https://www.pewresearch.org/religion/2025/02/26/decline-of-christianity-in-the-us-has-slowed-may-have-leveled-off.

10. Barna Group, "New Research: Belief in Jesus Rises, Fueled by Younger Adults," April 7, 2025, https://www.barna.com/research/belief-in-jesus-rises.
11. Barna Group, "Over Half of Gen Z Teens Feel Motivated to Learn More About Jesus," February 1, 2023, https://www.barna.com/research/teens-and-jesus.
12. Adam MacInnis, "Study: Gen Z Wants to Know More About Jesus," *Christianity Today*, October 26, 2022. https://www.christianitytoday.com/2022/10/gen-z-barna-research-survey-christian-faith-jesus.
13. United States Census Bureau, "History of Urban and Rural Areas," September 3, 2024, https://www.census.gov/about/history/historical-censuses-and-surveys/census-programs-surveys/geography/urban-and-rural-areas.html.
14. Oshin Aivazian, "UCLA: Birthplace of the Internet," UCLA, October 29, 1969, https://conferences.ucla.edu/ucla-birthplace-of-the-internet.
15. Leonard Kleinrock, "The First Message Transmission," ICANN, October 29, 2019, https://www.icann.org/en/blogs/details/the-first-message-transmission-29-10-2019-en.
16. Julian Ring, "30 Years Ago, One Decision Altered the Course of Our Connected World," *NPR*, April 30, 2023, https://www.npr.org/2023/04/30/1172276538/world-wide-web-internet-anniversary.
17. Meta, "What Is the Metaverse?," accessed June 7, 2025, https://about.meta.com/what-is-the-metaverse.
18. Sinem Buber, "The Most Regretted and Most Loved College Majors," *ZipRecruiter Blog*, November 3, 2022, https://www.ziprecruiter.com/blog/regret-free-college-majors.
19. Vijay Eswaran, "From Classroom to Career: Building a Future-Ready Global Workforce," World Economic Forum, December 16, 2024, https://www.weforum.org/stories/2024/12/from-classroom-to-career-building-a-future-ready-global-workforce/#:~:text=The%20World%20Economic%20Forum's%20Future,declining%20enthusiasm%20for%20traditional%20degrees.
20. *Merriam-Webster.com Dictionary*, s.v. "generation," accessed June 7, 2025, https://www.merriam-webster.com/dictionary/generation.
21. Ofer Tirosh, "What is The Fastest Growing Language?" Tomedes, March 27, 2024, https://www.tomedes.com/translator-hub/fastest-growing-languages.
22. English Proficiency Editorial Team, "English Language Statistics: A Comprehensive List," *English Proficiency*, October 19, 2023, https://englishproficiency.com/blog/english-language-statistics-a-comprehensive-list.
23. Simon Kemp, "Internet Use in 2024," DataReportal, January 31, 2024, https://datareportal.com/reports/digital-2024-deep-dive-the-state-of-internet-adoption#:~:text=There%20are%205.35%20billion%20people,the%20first%20time%20during%202023.
24. Pew Research Center, "Internet, Broadband Fact Sheet," November 13, 2024, https://www.pewresearch.org/internet/fact-sheet/internet-broadband.

25. Jennifer Huizen, "4 charts that show how much the role of phones has changed in the last 60 years," *InsideNova*, June 11, 2024, https://www.insidenova.com/news/national/4-charts-that-show-how-much-the-role-of-phones-has-changed-in-the-last/collection_c0fa6095-fb1f-5163-ab18-88ba7afee3c0.html?=/&subcategory=214%7CGig#2.
26. Michael H. Riordan, "Universal Residential Telephone Service," in *Handbook of Telecommunications Economics, Volume 1: Structure, Regulation, and Competition*, ed. Martin E. Cave (Amsterdam: Elsevier, 2002), 425. See https://www.columbia.edu/~mhr21/papers/US-aug-29.pdf.
27. Michael J. Coren, "Ethiopian Kids Hacked Their Donated Tablets In Just Five Months," Fast Company, December 7, 2012, https://www.fastcompany.com/2681011/ethiopian-kids-hacked-their-donated-tablets-in-just-five-months.
28. Ibid.
29. Lucy Tobin, "Slumdog Professor," *The Guardian*, March 2, 2009, https://www.theguardian.com/education/2009/mar/03/professor-sugata-mitra.
30. Omri Wallach, "Charted: U.S. Median House Prices vs. Income," *Visual Capitalist*, February 27, 2024, https://www.visualcapitalist.com/median-house-prices-vs-income-us/ .
31. Margaret Mead, "Generational Ties."
32. David Kinnaman, "Rising Spiritual Openness in America," Barna Group, January 18, 2023, https://www.barna.com/research/rising-spiritual-openness/.
33. *Cambridge Dictionary*, s.v. "disruption," accessed June 27, 2025, http://dictionary.cambridge.org/dictionary/english/disruption.
34. "The State of Church Attendance: Trends and Statistics [2025]," ChurchTrac, accessed June 11, 2025, https://www.churchtrac.com/articles/the-state-of-church-attendance-trends-and-statistics-2023.
35. George Santayana, *The Life of Reason, Introduction and Reason in Common Sense*, vol. 1, (New York: Charles Scribner's Sons, 1905), 172, PDF, accessed June 13, 2025, https://ratical.org/PandemicParallaxView/TheLifeOfReason-Santayana-1905.pdf.
36. Barna Group, "New Research: Belief in Jesus Rises, Fueled by Younger Adults."
37. Ibid.
38. Josephus, *The Antiquities of the Jews* 1.4.2, in *The Complete Works of Josephus*, trans. William Whiston (Thomas Nelson, 1998), 40.
39. The people of Ur worshipped the moon god, Sin. See Maddy Rager, "Abraham in the Bible-His Story and Significance," *Christianity.com*, February 11, 2025, https://www.christianity.com/wiki/people/what-learn-abraham-in-the-bible.html.
40. *Antiquities* 10.188
41. Bible Hub, "How do Daniel and Belteshazzar differ?" Accessed June 16, 2025, https://biblehub.com/q/how_do_daniel_and_belteshazzar_differ.htm.
42. United States Census Bureau, "New Data on Detailed Languages Spoken at Home and the Ability to Speak English," June 3, 2025, https://www.census.gov/newsroom/press-releases/2025/2017-2021-acs-language-use-tables.html.

43. Mohamad Moslimani and Jeffrey S. Passel, "What the Data Says about Immigrants in the U.S.," Pew Research Center, September 27, 2024, https://www.pewresearch.org/short-reads/2024/09/27/key-findings-about-us-immigrants.
44. The Editors of the Encyclopaedia Britannica, "Ziggurat," *Britannica*, May 16, 2005, https://www.britannica.com/technology/ziggurat.
45. Jaan Puhvel, "Cuneiform," *Britannica*, accessed June 16, 2025, https://www.britannica.com/topic/cuneiform.
46. Otto Neugebauer, *The Exact Sciences in Antiquity*, 2nd ed. (Dover Publications, 1969).
47. University of California Admissions, "UCLA: First-Year Admit Data," Accessed June 16, 2025, https://admission.universityofcalifornia.edu/campuses-majors/ucla/freshman-admit-data.html.
48. "UCLA Acceptance Rate, Admissions, SAT, ACT & GPA," Testbook, accessed June 16, 2025, https://testbook.com/en-us/college/university-of-california-los-angeles-admissions.
49. UCLA Financial Aid & Scholarships, "Cost of Attendance," Accessed June 16, 2025, https://financialaid.ucla.edu/how-aid-works/cost-of-attendance.
50. University of Southern California, *Undergraduate Financial Aid: Cost of Attendance 2024-2025*, accessed June 16, 2025, https://financialaid.usc.edu/undergraduate-financial-aid/cost-of-attendance/#chapter=2024-2025-estimate-of-cost-of-attendance.
51. Margaret Mead, "Generational Ties."
52. Clifford Grammich et al., *2020 U.S. Religion Census: Religious Congregations & Adherents Study* (Association of Statisticians of American Religious Bodies, 2023). See also https://www.usreligioncensus.org.
53. Pew Research Center, "In U.S. Decline of Christianity Continues at Rapid Pace," October 17, 2009, https://www.pewresearch.org/religion/2019/10/17/in-u-s-decline-of-christianity-continues-at-rapid-pace.
54. Clifford Grammich et al., *2020 U.S. Religion Census: Religious Congregations & Adherents Study.*
55. Joanne Beckman, "Religion in Post-World World II America," National Humanities Center, October 2000, https://nationalhumanitiescenter.org/tserve/twenty/tkeyinfo/trelww2.htm.
56. Jeffrey M. Jones, "U.S. Church Membership Falls Below Majority for First Time," Gallup, March 29, 2021, https://news.gallup.com/poll/341963/church-membership-falls-below-majority-first-time.aspx.
57. *Merriam-Webster.com Dictionary*, s.v. "syncretism," accessed June 17, 2025, https://www.merriam-webster.com/dictionary/syncretism.
58. Christian Smith and Melinda Lundquist Denton, *Soul Searching: The Religious and Spiritual Lives of American Teenagers* (Oxford University Press, 2005), 162-163.
59. "Daniel, the Prophet Who Was Not a Prophet," The Messianic Prophecy Bible Project, accessed June 17, 2025, https://www.messianicbible.com/feature/daniel-the-prophet-who-was-not-a-prophet.
60. Ibid.

61. Alyce Collins, "Gen Z Saving More of Their Money Than Any Other Generation," *Newsweek*, February 3, 2025, https://www.newsweek.com/gen-z-saving-more-money-other-generations-2023545.
62. Milly Tamati, "How to Win in the New Economy: Why Expert Generalists Are Uniquely Positioned to Succeed in This Era," Generalist World, June 10, 2024. https://www.generalistcareer.com/p/the-adaptive-economy.
63. Ibid.
64. Jonathan Rothwell, "Teens Spend Average of 4.8 Hours on Social Media Per Day," Gallup, October 13, 2023, https://news.gallup.com/poll/512576/teens-spend-average-hours-social-media-per-day.aspx.
65. NASA, "What Is Artificial Intelligence?," May 13, 2024, https://www.nasa.gov/what-is-artificial-intelligence.
66. OpenAI, *Chat GPT*, response to author's query.
67. Barna Group, "Three Takeaways on How Pastors Can Use AI," February 22, 24, https://www.barna.com/research/pastors-use-ai/#.
68. Ibid.
69. Margaret Mead, "Generational Ties."
70. WKRC, "Study Finds the Average American Spent 2.5 months on Their Phone in 2024," *Local 12*, January 10, 2025, https://local12.com/news/offbeat/study-cell-phone-smart-time-months-days-screen-amount-2024-2025-americans-average-finds-research-technology-mental-health-brain-iphone-android-tiktok-social-media-video-instagram-facebook-twitter-x.
71. See Unbabel Content Team, "What Happens to Your Brain When You Learn a New Language?," Unbabel February 19, 2019, https://unbabel.com/what-happens-to-your-brain-when-you-learn-a-new-language; Kendra Cherry, "How Neuroplasticity Works," Verywell Mind, May 17, 2024, https://www.verywellmind.com/what-is-brain-plasticity-2794886; Babbel, "What Happens to Your Brain When You Learn a Language," *YouTube* video, 2:56. Posted January 23, 2025, https://www.youtube.com/watch?v=7gAIL7mzPto; Hussna Mohamed, "How Speaking Multiple Languages Changes Your Brain," *DW*, May 5, 2025, https://www.dw.com/en/language-learning-brain-impact-explained-v2/a-72218512; Daniel Keane, "Screen Time Has Significant Long-Term Impact on Children's Brains," *The Standard*, November 17, 2023, https://www.standard.co.uk/news/health/screen-time-long-term-impact-childrens-brains-study-b1121006.html.
72. *Merriam-Webster.com Dictionary*, s.v. "integrate," accessed June 19, 2025, https://www.merriam-webster.com/dictionary/integrate.
73. Stephanie Susnjara and Ian Smalley, "What Is Blockchain?," IBM, accessed June 18, 2025, https://www.ibm.com/think/topics/blockchain.